MINIMUM **DESIGN**

Series directed by
Andrea Branzi

Philippe STARCK

Cristina Morozzi

24 ORE Cultura

Cover
Gun Lamp, Flos, 2005
© S+ARCK® Network, Paris

Published by
24 ORE Cultura srl

Editorial Director
Natalina Costa

Head of planning
Balthazar Pagani

Project Editor
Chiara Savino

Head of Iconographic
Gian Marco Sivieri

Head of Technical and Graphic
Maurizio Bartomioli
Graphic design and page layout
Irma Robbiati
Photolithography
Valter Montani

Editorial Assistant
Giorgia Montagna

With the contribution of

*Consultant Fund Raising
Coordination*
Chiara Giudice

Consultant Fund Raising
Anna Mainoli

Editing
Arianna Bassi
Silvia Russo

English translation
Sylvia Adrian Notini

First edition: November 2011

ISBN 978-88-6648-030-3

Printed in Italy

MINIMUM **DESIGN**

Titles in the series
Franco Albini
Ron Arad
Achille and Pier Giacomo Castiglioni
Joe Colombo
Tom Dixon
Alessandro Mendini
Jasper Morrison
Gio Ponti
Ettore Sottsass

Forthcoming titles
Alvar Aalto
Gae Aulenti
Mario Bellini
Andrea Branzi
Antonio Citterio
Michele De Lucchi
Stefano Giovannoni
Konstantin Grcic
Vico Magistretti
Angelo Mangiarotti
Enzo Mari
Carlo Mollino
Eero Saarinen
Marco Zanuso

CONTENTS

Philippe Starck

Andrea Branzi

Anyone wishing to understand the roots and appreciate the outstanding originality of Philippe Starck's work will need to begin with a look at the state of French design in the late 1980s: a composite state of things which brought together *decorateurs*, International Gothic tradition, aeronautical technology, *haute couture*, court intrigue and *arts and crafts* studios.

This was design based on a *stylistic* tradition, which found the Concorde to be the symbol of a new flying cathedral, the TGV the earth's answer to the aerospatial ogive, and Roger Tallon the official interpreter of design's *structural* side. Hence, tradition that was far-away and different from neoplastic compositions (spheres, cubes, lines, planes), and from the Calvinist rigour that most of Central European design had been founded on in the inter-war period. Although nowadays *globalization* tends to make local traditions disappear, with design headed in the direction of an internationalization of languages and cultures, the sources of Starck's work are still profoundly French. And perhaps we needn't stick to the eighties, as Starck actually began much earlier, in the seventies. Hence, these sources can be identified with the eighties, with the France of President Mitterand, who understood that for Paris to become the new capital of the European Union it first of all had to be the capital of Culture, and not just of the Louvre, the Musée D'Orsay, but also of the Beaubourg, new Cinema and new Design. When the President commissioned a young Starck to redesign his private quarters in the Elysée Palace the message he sent out was strong and clear (and no other country in Europe, including Italy,

would be capable of following suit), and it spoke of a season when culture was becoming a strategic part of a *nouveau grandeur* whose ambassadors in the world were philosophers, artists, film directors, and young designers. Philippe Starck was the finest representative of this new and ambitious season, but of past tradition as well: ogival forms, environmental sceneries, the relentless invention of new and unpredictable functions, design that was at once anti-design, theatre, urban decor. With instances of pure genius and self-irony, Starck anointed himself as the new King of Paris— and Court Jester.

In the tradition of the *maisons de haute couture* in Paris, Philippe Starck also stated a revolutionary principle vis-à-vis European *industrial* design: the designer's *brand* is more important than that of the company that produces his or her products. Starck thus took full hold of the media scene and the market. From the moment they were born his products were self-promotional, all that had to be done was to communicate them. The public recognized them and accepted the game that often distinguished them. It was a game made up of unpredictable and clever solutions both formally and in practical terms.

Unlike the New Italian Design of the 1970s (Alchimia and Memphis) from which Philippe Starck began the chase, his products were not experimental prototypes destined to small niche markets or to collectors; rather, they were products made in large series destined for large mass markets. Starck launched popular design. Their success was huge and unexpected, and

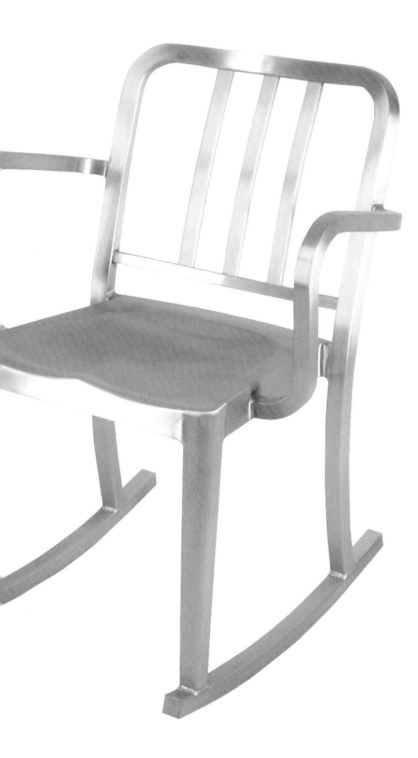

Heritage
Rocking Chair,
Emeco, 2000

sometimes even surprised the manufacturers themselves, whose *marketing* strategies hadn't picked up the profound changes that had come about in the market: the new market consisted of *exceptions, unpredictability, minorities*, where the concept of *normality* had essentially disappeared.

Philippe Starck lavished his creative energy (with some ups and down) not just on the world, but on every sector in the field of design: industrial design, architecture, cars, electronics, fashion, toys, interior design, entrepreneurship... Creative flexibility of this sort did not match the French industrial tradition, which was often unyielding and programmed around the average taste of mass distribution; this explains why Philippe Starck, especially in the 1990s, chose Italy as a productive interface. Starck also says that Italian industrialists are unique because they seem to know more about real quality and elegance. Although distant from the sophisticated and problematic themes and modalities of Italian design, Starck interpreted the network of Italian design industries almost as though they were the *agencies* for his *designer label*: Kartell, Alessi, Flos, Baleri, Driade, Cassina, Della Valle, Fluocaril, Duravit, Panzani, Aprilia; traditionally amenable industries, forever open to dealing with the *outside* rationale of the designers. And it is thanks to this very special encounter that they have enjoyed huge success both in terms of business and image, in some cases even breathing new life into the identity of plastic materials as well as complete ranges of products.

SPAGHETTERIA
PIZZERIA

IL CO

CAP

punta del
trattoio

caletta
delle Cote

la peraiola
dei gabbiani

cala
del
Fond

punta delle
Linguelle

cala
del
Moreto

punta
dello
Zenobio

cala
rossa

punta
del turco

cala
dei
porcili

Punta
del Capo

Punta
del
Patello

punta
della
cipitata

RIA·PIZZERIA·BIRRERIA·SPAGHE

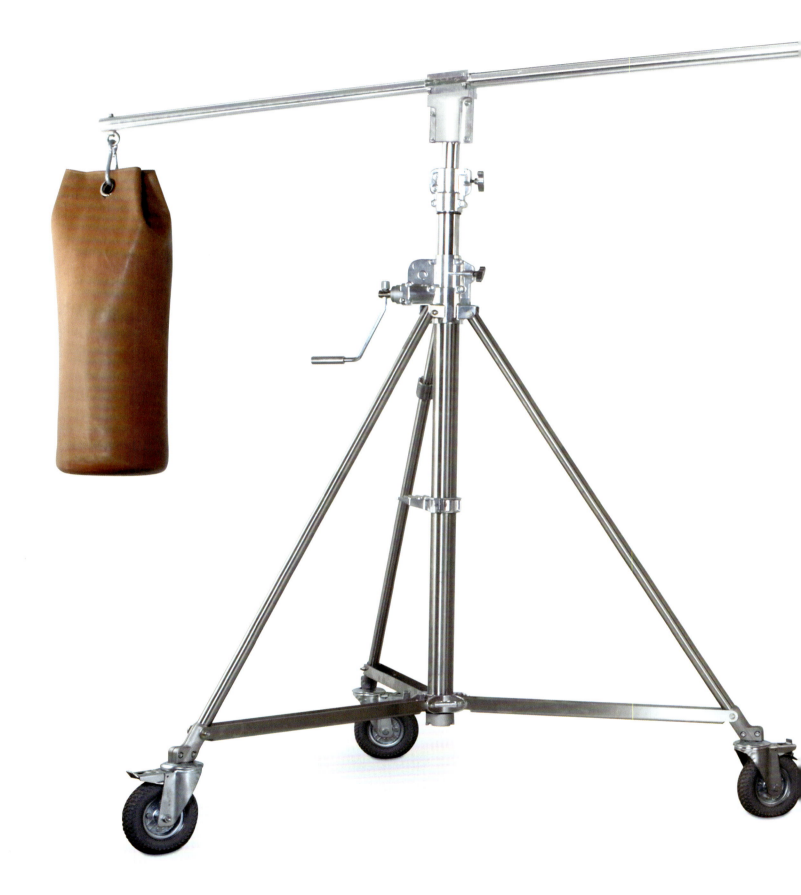

Marie Coquine,
for Maison Baccarat,
Paris, 2003

DEARS®

DEMOCRATIC
ECOLOGICAL
ARCHITECTURE
WITH RIKO
BY S+ARCK®

66 An ideal solution for Venetian water taxis, combining traditional Mahoganies with the utmost in technology. 99

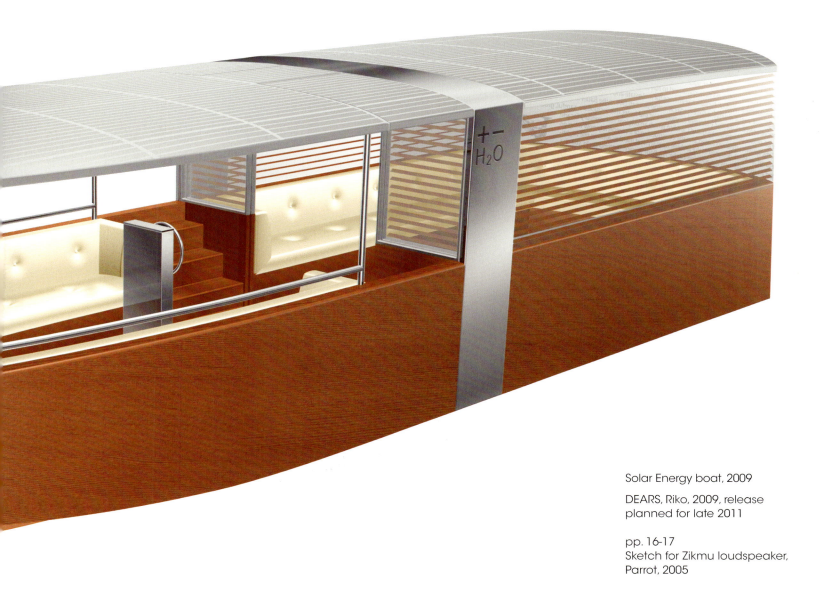

Solar Energy boat, 2009

DEARS, Riko, 2009, release planned for late 2011

pp. 16-17
Sketch for Zikmu loudspeaker, Parrot, 2005

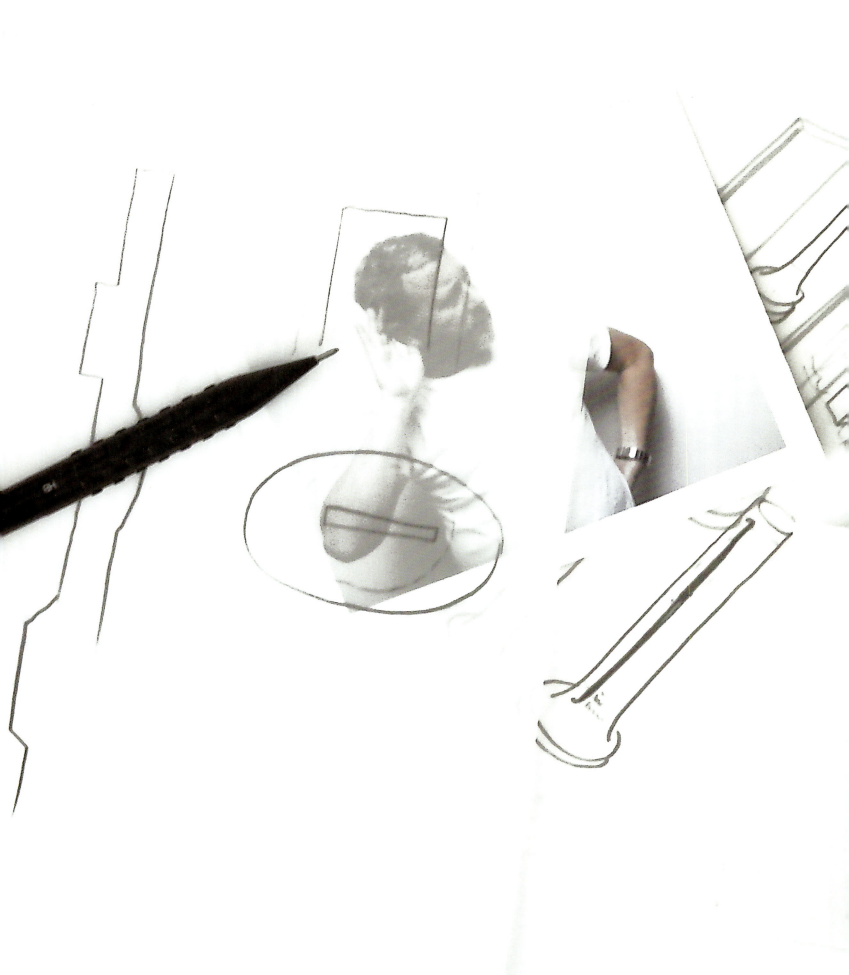

PARROT

BLUE TOOTH

Freebox, Free, 2010

p. 19
Photobooth,
Photomaton, 2010

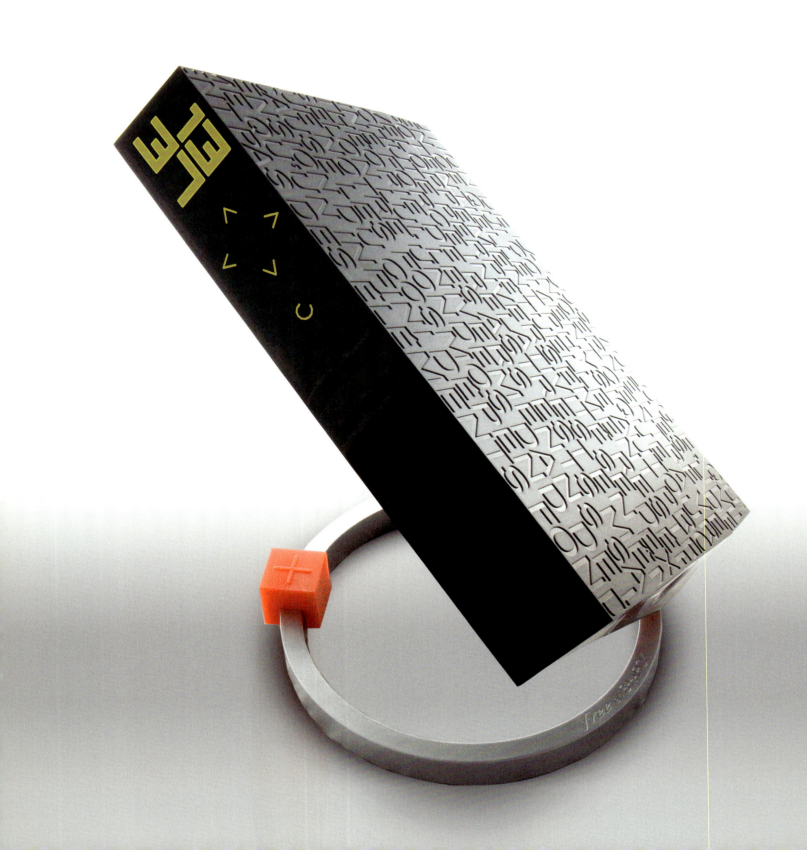

Seductive
Design

Thanks to Philippe Starck, design has crossed disciplinary boundaries to become a subject that's talked about, gradually rising to the role of cover story. People write about Philippe Starck the way they would about a star. He conquers the front pages of newspapers. Wherever he goes he makes the headlines. He is the undisputed star of design. Or, better still, he is the designer who invented "statization", which transformed design into legend. Christopher Pillet, who worked in his studio, observes that we are all indebted to Starck for having freed design from the "industrial aesthetic clad in a grey jacket and for having shown it the way to the star system and success stories" (*Petits enfants de Starck?* Paris: Dis Voir, 1999). When he appears he's hailed like a movie star. Journalists will queue up to interview him. In April 2007 in front of the Driade showroom in Via Manzoni motorcyclists (who founded the 6.5 Motoclub, named after the motorbike designed by

Starck, throughout Europe) sat waiting for him on their Motòs, designed for Aprilia in 1995, and applauded him like a champion when he arrived. Even the Italian comedy show *Zelig*, conducted by Claudio Bisio and Paola Cortellesi, used the designer for one of the sketches. In the very last episode (April 2011) comedian Giuseppe Giacobazzi did a monologue that parodied the design craze: "In my bathroom next to the shower there's a Philippe Starck clothes hook", he told the audience. "An aluminum hook that cost me 300 Euros…If I try to hang my terry cloth robe on it my wife shouts out: 'Not there! We won't be able to see the clothes hook!'" Roberto D'Agostino, an expert on what's new in fashion and the founder in 2000 of the gossip and news website Dagospia, says "you just can't be happy if you don't have an object by Starck in your house".
Christine Bauer, a professor at the University of Evry's Faculty of Communication Science, dedicated a

book to *Le cas Philippe Starck, ou De la construction de la notoriété* (Paris: L'Harmattan, 2001). For a whole year she perused the Starck archives, collecting all of the descriptions in the periodicals she could find: "A legend, an extraordinary combination of a pop star and a mad inventor"; "the star of French design transforms everything into design" [...]; "the Picasso of 1990 [...] Philippe Starck is to design what a cross between Marcel Duchamp and Andy Warhol is to art".

Alessandro Mendini says that Philippe Starck is a phenomenon. If only for the fact that he's a French designer because—as Starck also points out—"before him French designers just didn't exist". The French philosopher Michel Onfray writes that Starck's objects "create magic, they generate a strange fascination, they produce both ease and malaise, they cause changes to take place in the atmosphere. They can be inviting or keep you at a distance, but they never leave you indifferent, not even when you just take a furtive peek at them".

If you ask him what his secret is, he'll say: "My loquaciousness. Philosophers remain silent, so it's up to the designer to explain life and things". And Starck knows just how to use words to captivate his listeners, how to find interesting topics for discussion. He says that his projects are, first and foremost, excuses for telling stories and for creating liaisons, projects like Juicy Salif, his citrus-squeezer manufactured by Alessi, perhaps not the most efficient utensil of its kind, but an excellent way to start a conversation.

For his solo exhibition at Beaubourg in 2003, Starck published a pink leather-bound breviary with silver gilt-edged pages which contained a good reason for each one of his projects. About Marie, the chair he designed for Kartell, for example, he says: "I was able to do the most with the least: less material, hardly any material at all; less of a presence, in fact, it's completely see-through. And despite this, it provides maximum service: durability, lightness, stackability. It's an ageless object, an extremely honest, profoundly modern one. An almost ideal

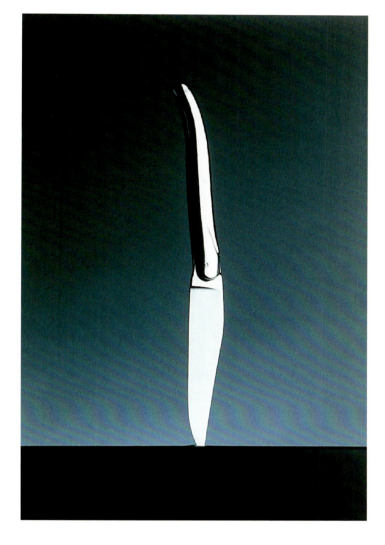

object. You can't see it because it's totally transparent. But if you do want to see it, then you'll realize that it's absolutely wonderful. Truly a technological exploit: with just one die-casting a transparent object!" About Miss Sissi, created for Flos (1998), he writes: "it's the start of a project based on collective memory. Sissi is a sort of commonplace. If you ask someone to name the first color that comes to mind they'll always say red; if you ask a child to name an animal, he or she will always name a lion or an elephant. If you ask someone to design a lamp then they design one like Miss Sissi, which was not designed by me, but by all of us together for our own great pleasure!"

A great *raconteur*, he knows how to be provocative, figuring out the desires of the ordinary person

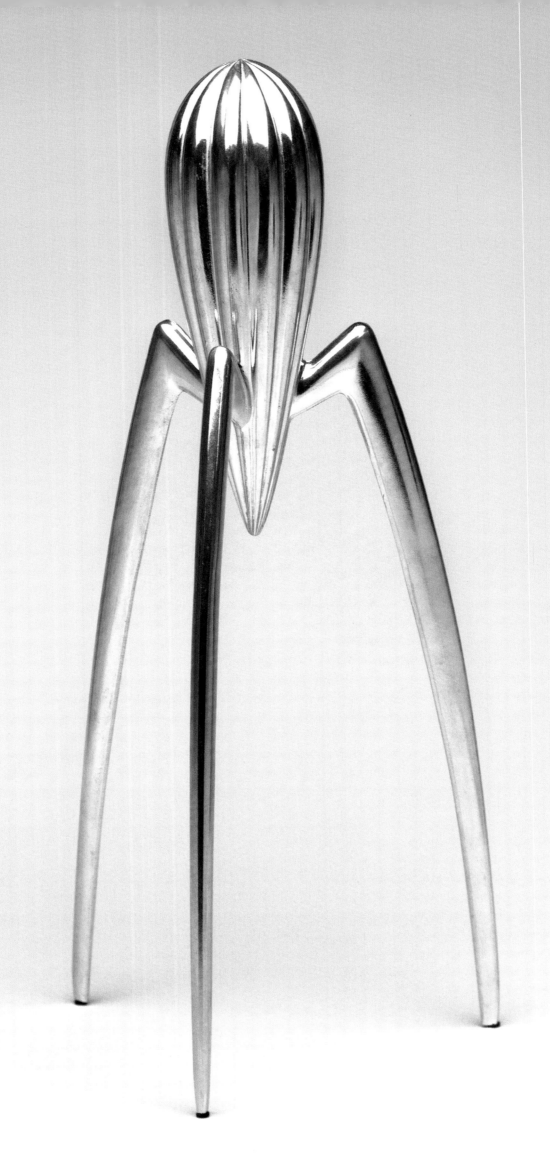

Juicy Salif,
Alessi, 1990

a split second before he or she is aware of it. He has dealt with ecology, food, luxury, simplicity and always at just the right moment, a little ahead of the times, but not too much so. He says he was the first to talk about ethics, democracy in design, political and subversive action with his wooden houses that come in a kit (La maison des 3 suisses), or with his catalogue of good products *Good Goods*. He complied with women by declaring that design was becoming feminized. He used his art to cause shock waves, designing Guns, 2007, for Flos, a series of table lamps whose base is actually a golden Kalashnikov: "A manifesto against war", he said. And so he provided yet another topic for discussion. The magazine *Domus* (issue nos. 880 and 881, April and May 2007) has devoted as many as two editorials to his work, assembling both the pros and cons of his work according to designers and critics. Also provocative was his soft furniture series Collection Privé for Cassina unveiled at the 2007 Milan Furniture Fair, conceived in order to make sex easier. "I became aware", said Starck at the crowd-filled press conference in the showroom in Via Durini", of a glaring inconsistency. Sex is everywhere today. All you have to do is open a magazine or turn on the TV; but oddly enough in the home there is no piece of furniture devoted to sex. We have the right to sit down, eat, sleep, but it's as if we didn't have the right to make love, except in the bedroom. I decided that this inconsistency needed to be solved and because I'm obsessed with sex I based the project on my own personal experience and designed a collection that favours a woman's comfort while she's having sex". Perhaps the main reason for his widespread success is precisely the fact that he attaches so much importance to people. And then there's his skill at observing, even though he tries to spend as much time as possible in secluded places, in any one of his many homes. Hence, honesty, generosity, tenderness, qualities unhesitatingly seen in him by Brigitte Bury who insisted on having him as the architect for the Maison Baccarat in Paris, one of his masterpieces; she describes him as "a visionary, a humanist, somewhat impertinent; a pure boy who chooses to work only for those he loves". Starck was introduced to Italy by Enrico Baleri, who first met him at Milan's Galleria Marconi in 1982, on the occasion of the unveiling of Mario Botta's Seconda chair for Alias, the company he had set up in 1979 together with Marilisa Baleri Decimo, Carlo and Francesco Forcolini. "The jacket he had on was something a beggar might wear, but he was also wearing Eau Lente, the very sophisticated fragrance made by Diptyque. He had a book of very bold designs with him that I really liked. I saw him again in Paris in 1984 at the Disegno shop in rue de Renard directed by Arturo dal Punta, who had become his guardian angel, and I came back to Italy with a design for the chair Francesca Spanish". Enrico Baleri still has the first book about Starck, written by Christine Colin and published by Mardaga in 1988; the autograph dedication reads: "Pour Enrico Baleri, l'homme qui a fait de moi un designer italien". It was actually thanks to Enrico Baleri that I was able to meet Philippe Starck. I had read an article in the weekly *Elle* (French edition) about the furniture he had designed for François Mitterand's private quarters in the Elysée Palace and I decided that I wanted to interview him for the magazine *Modo*. I went to see him in 1985 in Montfort-l'Amoury, where he was living in a period residence at the edge of the Forest of Rambouillet. I was his guest there for a week which we spent in the merry company of other friends, talking very little about design, drinking lots of champagne and eating delicious Breton crabs. We would have candlelight dinners in the kitchen. None of the furniture was designer except for the Aeo by Cassina, but the lights were dimmed. And even then the people who lived there would say as he walked by "ah Starck!" I went back to Monfort with Enrico Baleri a year later in January in freezing weather (the temperature was - 12 C.) We were frozen when we got there and had with us a piece of Parmesan cheese, his favourite, which we had bought at an Italian deli in rue du Bac. Spending time in his house and at his dinner table helped me to understand him and his work much more than any discussion on theory. I understood that the secret behind his objects that know how to please the viewer even when they are very distant from current taste lies in his greatest gift of all: his sense of the quality of life, which is not a question of material things, of the ostentation of beautiful features, but of well-being and the pleasure of the senses—taste and smell included. Starck has a nose for what the future has in store because he has a very refined ability to recognize odours, fragrances: you can walk past him and he'll tell you what perfume you've "got on"—and he's never wrong. I understood that by blending apparently unrelated objects he manages to create surprising, but always inviting atmospheres, where surprise is combined with being at one's ease, where dissonances become harmony.

Telling Stories

People like the objects Starck designs, even when they're not functional, because they're seductive. Khaslavsky and Shedroff believe that: "Seduction is a process. It gives rise to a rich and compelling experience that lasts over time". They say that the three basic phases are enticement, connection and satisfaction. To illustrate their theory Khaslavsky and Shedroff analysed Philippe Starck's citrus- squeezer Juicy Salif (Alessi 1990) whose design was first sketched on a paper napkin in a pizzeria on an island near Capraia, Tuscany. Donald A. Norman tells the story in his book *Emotional Design. Why We Love (or Hate) Everyday Things* (New York: Basic Books, 2004). "I'll buy it", he says, "That was pure visceral reaction. The juicer is indeed bizarre, but delightful. Why? Fortunately, Khaslavsky and Shedroff have done the analysis for me. [...] It promises to make an ordinary action extraordinary. It also promises

Attila Stool, Kartell,
1999

p. 31
Miss Sissi, Flos, 1990

to raise the status of the owner to a higher level of sophistication for recognizing its qualities. [...] While the juicer doesn't necessarily teach the user anything new about juice or juicing, it does teach the lesson that even ordinary things in life can be interesting and that design can enhance living. It also teaches to expect wonder where it is unexpected [...]". Philippe Starck in *Starck Explications* published by the Centre Georges Pompidou on the occasion of his solo show uses an anecdote to tell us about it: "One day a young bride received the first visit from her mother-in-law. She felt a bit uneasy and didn't know what to talk about. One of the gifts she'd received was a Juicy Salif citrus-squeezer. Her mother-in-law asks: 'What exactly is this object?' She describes her juicer and the conversation begins. Contact is made between women whom we don't expect to be fond of each other". One of Philippe Starck's greatest talents is his ability to use words and objects to tell stories. And he placed this talent on show, theatrically, for his solo exhibition at the Centre Georges Pompidou curated by Marie Laure Jousset (Paris, 26 February - 21 May 2003). The exhibition caused quite a stir. Some people asked to have their ticket refunded because there was nothing to see, or, better still, touch! In the dark elliptical 800-square-metre room, surrounded by grey velvet curtains all you could see were the images of his objects and displays as they ran by on the eleven screens placed above his talking effigy. Starck's many faces moved their lips in a ceaseless murmur and bat their eyelids to recount, one by one, the projects of his lightning-fast career. At the centre all you could see was a large Shadow, an oversized object made of bronze that materialized the creator's "gigantic" unconscious. At the entrance a clown mask drew the visitors in by crying out: "Enter! Enter! There's nothing to see, but lot's to learn!" The surprising representation was much better than a host of theories at telling the visitors about the fate of goods. Starck is convinced that design concerns life, that it must be accessible to as many people as possible, that it must

circulate along the sales channels and be used in everyday life and not just displayed in museums. And for his solo show he chose to leave his objects in the places they were meant for, and to instead bring himself to the museum, along with his idea of design and his methodology. Hence, he would not use his objects to carry his message, but would instead talk directly to the public, revealing in the quiet of a dark room the backstage scenes of his successes and his failures, without ever taking himself seriously, picturing himself in big statues that were meant to be torn down as icons. He used an alluring voice to seduce, to show that his design is, first and foremost, storytelling, and to say that his objects are the materialization of the enchantment of words.

This theatrical show was a pivotal point in the historiography of design. By inviting visitors to the museum to consume only words and images, by stressing the fact that the spectacle of goods belongs to stores and shopping malls, to markets and to places where life circulates and time passes and not to museum spaces, not to abstract places where time is instead suspended, Starck provided a fascinating and definitive answer to the sterile debate about whether design should have its own museums and be available to consumers in shop windows. Always true to what he believes, he chose not to have a catalogue and in its place conceived a book of definitions, a sort of compendium of his ideas on everyday things and how to make them attractive to as many people as possible. "To me that exhibition", declared Starck, "is a balance that I wish to be critical, and it's the chance to say what I have never said. How I've wanted to break the balls of the rich, how I've wanted to break the balls of the institutions, how I've wanted to break the balls of poor living. I'm an irritator. I want to show people who my real targets are. I've always had enemies and they represent money, luxury, oppression, fascism, male chauvinism, lack of elegance, fake products, fake prices". (C. Morozzi, *Interni*, 2003).

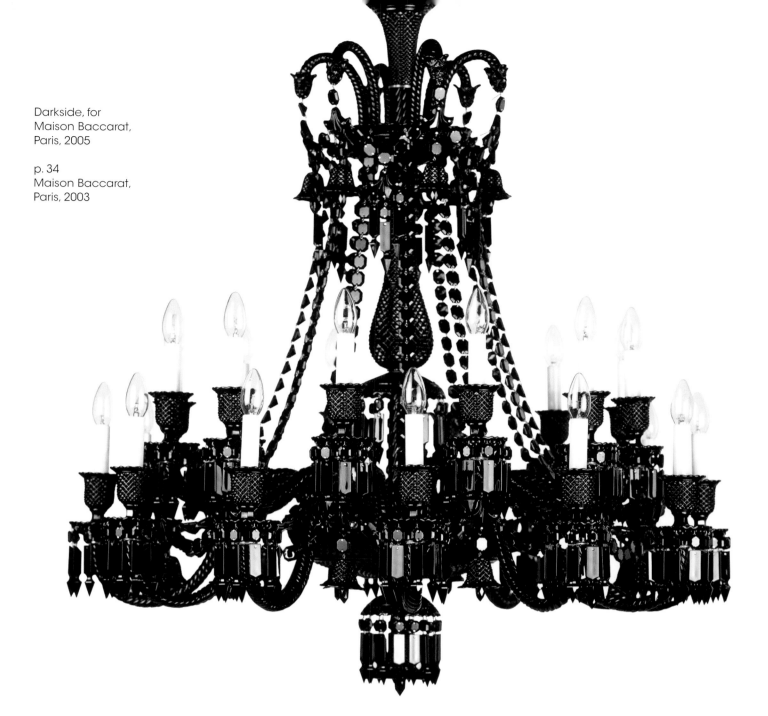

Darkside, for
Maison Baccarat,
Paris, 2005

p. 34
Maison Baccarat,
Paris, 2003

The Starck Style

Philippe Starck's style cannot be classified as part of any of the trends used to establish common denominators, which may be useful in putting multifarious contemporary production in order. Starck has contributed to making design popular, transforming the term into a sort of "suitcase" that can be adapted to the most varied of contexts, making it a precious attribute and not just the definition of a method and a process. Thanks to him, having a designer object in one's home has become as desirable as wearing the latest fashion. Starck possesses his own style, he says so himself: "my only style is freedom, but of course my creations have some limits in common, since they come from the same brain". His style is immediately recognizable, even if each time it is expressed in different formal results. Styling has nothing to do with it, he doesn't strum a single chord to create fascinating bodywork the way exponents of streamlining do; each time he reinvents objects, breathing new life into a repertoire of endless variety. Although we recognize his products, they are never "in the style of..." There is something alien about the objects, never-before-seen, at times even disturbing. They are strong signs characterized by an almost magical power, capable of capturing the attention and the admiration of the most diverse categories of people. In order to introduce design into the society of communication, to make it a popular phenomenon akin to rock music, Starck

Clockwise: Naked Shoes
Starck, Puma Shoes,
2005; O-Ring watch,
Starck Watch with Fossil,
2006; Samsonite by
Starck, 2000

Hard Drive,
LaCie, 2009

works just like a body artist, using the body as the medium to represent the changes in the figure of the designer and the status of design. He represents himself as Shiva, with six arms each holding a different object: six different typologies, from shoes to lighting fixtures, to a bottle of mineral water, thus illustrating the variety of his interventions (1998 cover of his *Good Goods* catalogue). He poses wearing a plaid jacket and a Napoleonic bicorne cocked to one side (photo by Jeff Reidel); hanging from a hook along with a series of Faitoo table and kitchen accessories by Alessi (J.B. Mondino, 1996); wearing a chef's hat and armed with a knife and fork to publicize the restaurant Bon in rue de La Pompe in Paris (2000); bare-chested and with his head in the opposite direction on the cover of the book *Starck* published by Taschen in 2003. Although they are made by different companies,

all of his products unmistakably show his hallmark. Starck has transformed his sign into a brand that has the strength of a fire-brand. He understands that people don't need more design; they need the immediate emotions and magic of objects of desire and not of utility. He has generated all around himself a great deal of professional uproar because, as Bruce Sterling, a critic and one of the greatest representatives of cyberpunk, once said "he has understood that what can't be overcome with reason can be subverted with clamor. This is what the glamour of design is for" (*Shaping Things*, Cambridge: MIT Press, 2005).
"I work to be loved", were Philippe Starck's words at the *Essere benessere* show organized by *Interni* for the 2000 Milan Triennale. "To deserve to exist, to have a place on this earth. Creating good objects that can lead to the well-being of others. My objects that

Maclaren baby
stroller, 2006

make people feel good are the exchange goods I use to be loved by people...My work is to bring well-being. Work makes sense if it succeeds in sending love" (C. Morozzi, *Interni,* 2000). His great quality is to transform the everyday object into something special, unique, capable of satisfying the consumer's subliminal expectations; this means bestowing on what is normal not just functional values (after all functionality is taken for granted), but the capacity to express messages of love, tenderness, humour, politics, and so on. Starck doesn't see himself as an artist, but rather as a creator capable of pulling out surprises that are ever fertile, he being an explorer of new ideas. The philosopher Michael Onfray says that Starck transfigures the real and eliminates the separation between the museum object and the everyday object. With him, thanks to him, we can experience our houses as though they were museums" (V. Guillaume (ed.), *Scritti su Starck*, Milan: Postmedia, 2004). His objects are invented, and yet they immediately seem familiar thanks to the ability he shows in using morphological citations borrowed from nature, anatomy, geology, osteology. Starck redeems tradition and kitsch and boldly dares to be a citationist without, however, being cacophonic. He shapes forms never seen before, immediately alluring ones, thanks to his ability to distil the essence of each typology which he then transforms with the incisiveness of his sign into something new and surprising, but capable all the same of being familiar and friendly. With Philippe Starck design is no longer a science, rather it becomes science fiction, the reign of the imaginary par excellence. The difference is that his imaginary objects are possible and not just fiction. At the beginning there's a great interest in "us" humans, in the great history of our evolution and our mutation; in the forms of what is real, a wisdom in looking beyond appearances, an amused glance at human events and a sense of the hyperbole that leads him to transfigure everyday things. "Against

the tyranny of straight lines", writes Michel Onfray, "horizontals and verticals, against the empire of abscissas and ordinates, of geometry and math, Starck sets in motion the seductive curvaceousness of biology and bionics, the sinewy line, the curved volume, the playful protuberance, the voluptuous line, the joyful form, the extravagant diagonal, the mysterious fold, the unexpected construction" (V. Guillaume, *op. cit.*). Starck possesses a mythical sense of design which he uses like the sceptre of a demiurge to bestow upon the surrounding world a seductive and perverse image, capable of drawing upon the primary emotions, the ones that touch the stomach before they do the mind. His design has become popular because it speaks a pre-verbal language that goes straight to the heart and the gut. His things speak, ask questions, entreat the user, they demand his or her attention, they make them smile or feel surprise. "In Starck's game", Onfray continues, "objects are humanized and human beings are objectified, animals are mineralized, and plants become like humans" (V. Guillaume, *op. cit.*). If we consider the reflections of the French sociologist Michel Maffesoli, we might risk classifying the objects designed by Starck with the dominion of Hermès, which alludes to singularity, exception, hedonism. More than products these are "mental things", objects, not just functional, but charged with an extraordinary force that gives them a special aura. "The objects that belong to the dominion of Hermès", Maffesoli says, "have the quality and the beauty that can be found in the rooms of primitive art museums that represent the roots of our collective unconcious [...] they have a symbolic function, that is, they are creations capable of mobilizing the dream, the game and the imaginative side of the human being [...] these are objects that summon up the depth of sensibility, the need for singularity, the need to be surrounded by beautiful things" (Michel Maffesoli, *Iconologies, nos idol@tries postmodernes,* Paris: Albin Michel, 2008).

Miss K, Flos, 2003

P. 41
Miss Lacy,
Driade, 2007

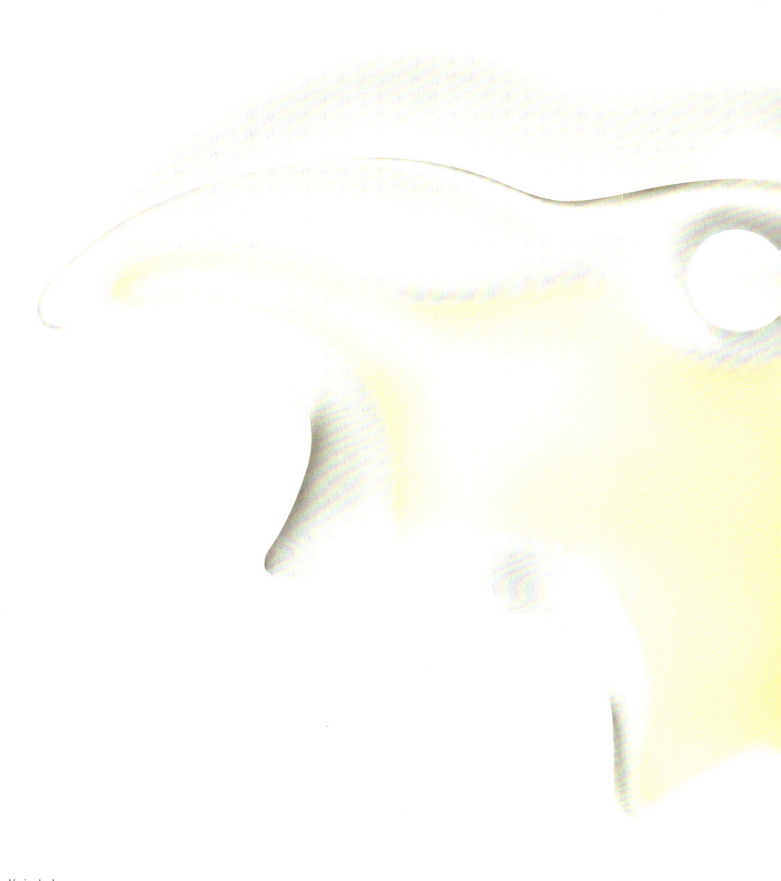

L'air du temps
perfume, Nina
Ricci, 2010

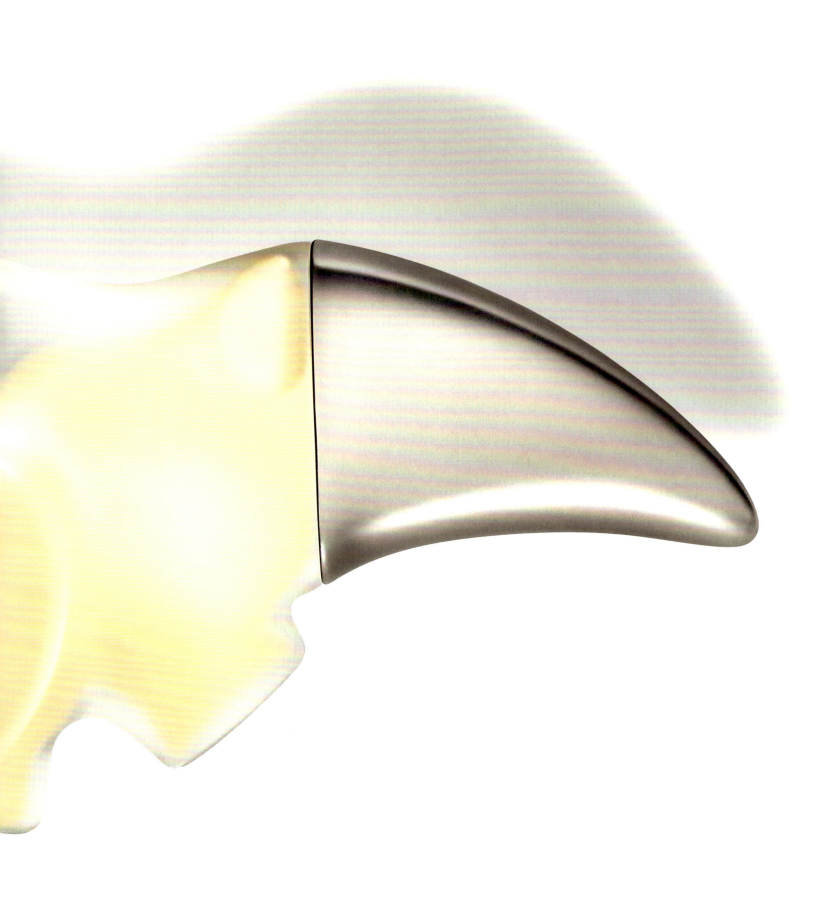

Catalogue of Objects
A selection of products created by Philippe Starck

CAFÉ COSTES

OAO

MISS SISSI

VIRTUELLE

JUICY SALIF

TV JIM NATURE

A YACHT

VIRGIN GALACTIC

1967 ———— 1999 ————

COLLECTION DE CRISE

WW STOOL

MOTO 6.5 APRILIA

ATTILA STOOL

MARIE COQUINE

MAISON BACCARAT

KNIFE

CHILDREN'S TOOTHBRUSH

LOUIS GHOST

HERITAGE ROCKING CHAIR

MISS K

GOOD GOODS

MARIE

SAMSONITE BY STARCK

A TENDERS

44

GUN LAMP

HOME GYM OFFICE

75-METRE YACHT

NAKED SHOES STARCK

HARD DRIVE

PERSONAL WIND TURBINE

PORTE HELICOPTÈRE

DARKSIDE

MACLAREN

MI MING

SOLAR ENERGY BOAT

L'AIR DU TEMPS

LOU READ

2005 ——————— 2009 ——————— 2011 |

H+

O-RING WATCH

MISS LACY

MAMA SHELTER HOTEL

LIGHT PHOTON

NET

LULU S+ARCK® EYES

ZIKMU

MR. IMPOSSIBLE

HC+

STARCK WITH BALLANTYNE

ZARTAN

SUPER NAKED XV

LAN RESTAURANT

PRIVÉ COLLECTION

LA FEUILLE D'EAU

The Objects

GOOD GOODS CATALOGUE

Year: 1993

Distribution: La Redoute

In compliance with his Democratic Design, which means providing the very best to as many people as possible while at the same time keeping prices down, in 1993 Philippe Starck signed a contract with La Redoute, a large mail-order firm and number one in France today for the online sale of clothing and household goods, to create a catalogue that would suggest something different, far from the whims of the latest fashions: *Good Goods* is a collection of "non-products for the non-consumers of the future moral market". The catalogue consists of a sober A4 format and the cover is the work of the much-acclaimed photographer Jean-Baptiste Mondino as requested by Philippe Starck, showing a strange being of nondescript age and mixed-gender whose bald head indicates intelligence, third eye mid forehead says that it can see what others can't, and whose tiny white beard symbolizes Far Eastern wisdom. *Good Goods* is not a catalogue of trendy commercial products, it's a catalogue of objects needed by consumers whom Starck has dubbed "non-consumers", i.e. non-reactionary people who are very different from those who have always feared the future. With this project Starck was one of the first to deal with the issues of the ethics and morality of products, and he did so much before these became marketing subjects. The aim of *Good Goods* is to make good products, that is, products that truly provide a service, known. The collection is made up of a vast series of products designed by Starck, including organic cotton clothing, non-toxic paint, and so on, as well as objects he personally selected, such as an antigas mask to be used as protection against bacteriological accidents.

OAO

Year: 1993

Company: Lima Expert

"The most direct way to intervene upon life is to deal with nutrition", Starck says, "that's why I decided to create a company that produces biological and organic food. I tried to make biological and organic food more accessible and above all sort of sexy. To do so I followed a very simple rule. I created packaging for food, much like the kind that's used to sell cosmetics, so that people who are undecided will go to a store and say: "How beautiful! What is this package? It's whole grain rice. Well then I'll try some whole grain rice. They say it's healthy!" I think that if you fill your body up with good fuel it'll work better and so will your brain. The brain has to work well so that intelligence will develop, especially because intelligence generates love. So even whole grain rice can be something that helps people to love others". The range of OAO products represents a creative and modern approach to organic nutrition. Its biological wholeness is guaranteed by the Lima Expert laboratory, a forerunner in the organic food business, which has been guaranteeing a rigorous selection of its biological food products for over forty years. Among the first to sell organic champagne in France.

ORGANIC COMPACT FOOD
Couscous aux légumes et à la coriandre
3 min. instant

ORGANIC COMPACT FOOD
Pâtes aux cèpes parfumées à la truffe blanche
4 min. instant

ORGANIC COMPACT FOOD
Pâtes aux petits légumes et au basilic
3 min. instant

CHAMPAGNE
Jean-Pierre Fleury
Sélectionné par OAO
BRUT
75cl   12%vol
Contrôle Ecocert

ORGANIC SPAGHETTI

ORGANIC TOMATO SAUCE
Basilic

ATLANTIC SEA SALT

OLIO EXTRA VERGINE
DI OLIVA BIOLOGICA
SAN VITO

ORGANIC TOMATO SAUCE
Mexican

VIRTUELLE

Year: 1994

Commissioned by Carlo Perrone

It was a request made by Carlo Perrone, grandson of the Vicomtesse de Noailles and a great patron of the arts, that prompted Starck to study the aesthetics of a sail yacht, a revolutionary one resembling an iridescent spindle where the most advanced technologies are combined with a traditional, reassuring image. The sailboat's elegant, sleek line is the result of the great effort made by the designer to reduce and pare down. Preformed teak was used to finish the exterior. For the interior, what looks like mahogany is really carbon fibre composite. Starck chose advanced, ultrasophisticated, extremely lightweight materials for the interior, ones that are ideal for sailing boats, such as aluminium diamond plate and carbon fibre composite. Yet, in spite of the fact that cutting-edge materials were used to make it, Virtuelle has all the codes of the classic

sailing yacht. Thanks to the work of expert naval engineers Virtuelle sails smoothly and wins races, but at the same time its image refers to the traditional codes of navigation. It was the first boat with a grey hull—which until then had always been white.

LOUIS GHOST

Year: 1999

Company: Kartell

Material: clear or mass-coloured polycarbonate

This comfortable, transparent, stackable armchair, a smiling revisitation of Louis XV style, is a bold example of injected polycarbonate in a single mould. "After Marie" (also for Kartell), Starck says, "a chair I consider to be almost perfect, but that perhaps precisely because of its extreme purity is a bit too abstract, I started toying with the idea of making a one-mould polycarbonate chair; a highly technological, stackable, totally transparent chair, but with more humanity. To do that, I thought at the time,

I was going to have to add a touch of the past. So I created a medallion chair. A Louis something-or-other...which actually resembles the shadow a chair like that would cast. I called it Louis Ghost. Technologically speaking it's one of the most advanced in the world. While culturally it represents the successful binomial of technology and collective memory, but made lighter by the citation".
Louis Ghost is the perfect example of Starckian Democratic Design.

YACHT A

Year: 2002

Shipbuilder: TKMS AG Blohm&Voss GmbH, Kiel

This 119-metre-long megayacht is characterized by its natural design in the shape of a fish. Its lines blend right in with the sea world. The simplified, sleek appearance, the advanced technological solutions which allow for the natural integration of the boat in its element, lead to an ecological type of approach to boat design. The calibrated harmony of the proportions makes it hard to assess the boat's dimensions at first sight. Perfect down to the tiniest detail, it took five years of hard work to fine-tune it. The yacht's design stems from Starck's instinctive approach: clearly stating that he's not a naval engineer, he defines A an "ecological project because it doesn't leave a footprint in nature; it sails as smooth as oil never raising the waves, and can even achieve over 25 knots". He doesn't describe it as something that's made from steel, aluminium, and so on, but as something designed with philosophy. The interior is arranged in open, loft-like spaces, for life at sea without separations. The most innovative technology for A was actually realized with the most traditional of materials: teak. Teak Solutions specially developed 23-metre-long teak planks for it.

A TENDERS,
LIMOUSINE AND OPEN

Year: 2003

Built in Australia

"Megayacht A", writes Starck, "was designed to harmonize with the waves, the sea and with the people who experience the sea. Philippe Starck also created some of the most stylish tenders to complement the 119-metre superyacht 'A' to ferry her guests ashore. The two 11-metre custom-designed tenders are regarded as two solid examples of cutting-edge design and engineering. The 11-metre Limousine Tender is a stunning personalized transport vehicle with beautifully varnished teak. The sophisticated interior can match many mainline superyachts, with 1.9 metres of headroom, entertainment systems, air-conditioning and refrigeration. The state-of-the-art tender has remotely activated, hydraulically powered hatches, and retractable navigation systems. An 11-metre open-top service tender, the Open Tender houses a circular guest compartment at the centre in order to cruise around the superyacht and access other amenities positioned in the bow and sides. The two tenders have a completely new aesthetic that stems from the elegance of intelligence.

VIRGIN GALACTIC

Graphic design studio: GBH Design Ltd, for the logo

Creative director: Philippe Starck

Year: 2004 (First presented on 13 December 2005)

Company: Virgin Galactic

Richard Branson chose Philippe Starck as the creative director of this great new adventure, investing him with a sort of mission: to be the guardian of the temple of a new cult, that is, freedom of space. Carrying out this mission came naturally to Starck: Virgin Atlantic signifies the liberalization of space, until now the exclusive property of the military. In short, this means the democratization of space. Indeed, prices are expected to go down after the first flights have taken place. Starck's chief aim is the democratization of resources. The logo is that of the human iris. "A spirit of adventure and curiosity are both related to vision", Starck explains. The cloudy iris signifies the chance to look, for the first time, at the earth from the

space of our eyes. The pupil incorporates the embryo of something new, unique, but accessible. Something far and away, yet close too. The design for the spaceport's final logo was meant to include the image of the founder of Virgin Atlantic Sir Richard Branson's own iris. The logo symbolically expresses a vision of the future. Hence, it is perfect, according to Branson's enthusiastic comment, for representing this new chapter in the history of space navigation that we have been dreaming about since we were children. The incisiveness of the image transcends the simple representation of the chance for just anyone to travel in space, and alludes to the force of the spirit that pushes human thresholds further and further forward.

GUN LAMP

Year: 2005 (project from 2002)

Company: Flos

Materials: gold-plated aluminium alloy, laminate paper, black shade

When the controversial Gun Lamp, with its gilt aluminium base shaped like a Kalashnikov, was unveiled at the 2005 Euroluce event in Milan it came with a pamphlet written by Philippe Starck explaining the symbolic value of the project: "To Life, to Death...Life itself doesn't have much value—life and death become mistaken for one another, almost by accident, with no importance. But we are making every effort. A civilization has been created so that life can live....The great, beautiful life, guaranteed for all, has thrived and survived until today, the 21st century, the third millennium of civilized civilization. Well done, rest in peace. Boom! It's never what you think. After a cycle of enlightenment the darkness returns, swift, dense, menacing. We go backward, death lies in wait. Today we kill. Religiously. Militarily. Civilly. We kill out of ambition, greed. We kill for the fun of it. For the show...We live in Banana Republics", Starck continued, "our masters are tyrants. Designed, manufactured, sold, dreamed, purchased and used, weapons are our new icons. Our lives are only worth a bullet. The Gun Collection is nothing other than a sign of the times. We have the symbols we deserve. Glory to our dictators, to life and to death". Starck has determined that 20% of sales from the lamp shall be donated to the "Brotherhood of Man", a non-governmental European organization that promotes and supports programmes for social and economic development in favour of diadvantaged populations. *Domus* dedicated two separate editorials (no. 880 April 2005 and no. 881 May 2005) to the Gun Lamp with comments by notable critics and designers. The Gun Lamp comes in three versions: a small table lamp with a base in the shape of a Beretta, representing weapons manufactured in Europe; a large table lamp with a stem that resembles a Kalashnikov AK-47, alluding to Soviet-produced weapons; and, lastly, a floor lamp (Lounge Gun) with a support that resembles an M-16 rifle , indicating weapons made in the United States. The gilt finish on the weapons presumably alludes to the relationship between war and money; the black lampshade represents death and the tiny crosses carved inside the black diffuser are an invitation to remember the dead.

Kalashnikov
AK-47, Gun
Lamp, Flos,
2005

Rifle M-16, Gun Lamp,
Flos, 2005

p. 66
Beretta, Gun Lamp,
Flos, 2005

H+,
HYDROGEN CAR

Year: 2005 (Model)

Material: polyurethane finished with integrated leather

This is a manifesto project that signals a willingness to produce objects for the benefit of our civilization's evolution. This means making the most with the least material, that is, moving in the direction of a gradual dematerialization.
The search for new technologies is an answer to people's real needs (today's cars don't need to go 200 km/hour) and not to the made-up ones induced by the multinationals, accomplices in the periodic changes in styles. "A hydrogen car, for example", Starck says, "will naturally take its place on the market as an inevitable transportation solution".

H+ by S+ARCK®

LULU, S+ARCK® EYES
EYEWEAR

Year: 2005

Brand: S+ARCK® EYES

Produzione: Alain Mikli

Because sight is man's most important sense Philippe Starck and Alain Mikli, the eccentric French spectacles manufacturer, have invented "the eyeglasses of the future", that is, Biovision. What's new about these eyeglasses is the biomechanical mechanism that allows the temples to move the same way a human collarbone does. In short, thanks to a special screw-less hinge, the unique flexibility of these glasses assures constant pressure on the temples, and provides for better comfort. Wearing a pair of "Starck Eyes" becomes the height of naturalness: the wearer doesn't perceive the presence of the frames, but just the benefit of the lenses that can be dark or graded. Once more Starck has invented a system that makes material adaptable and not invasive. Patented the world over, in compliance with Starck's philosophy, these eyeglasses harmonize and valorize the physiognomy of the person wearing them, thereby avoiding applying a logo to his or her face as well.

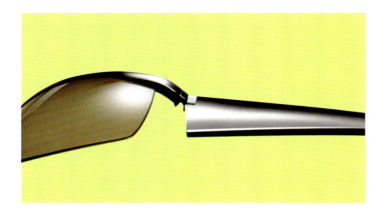

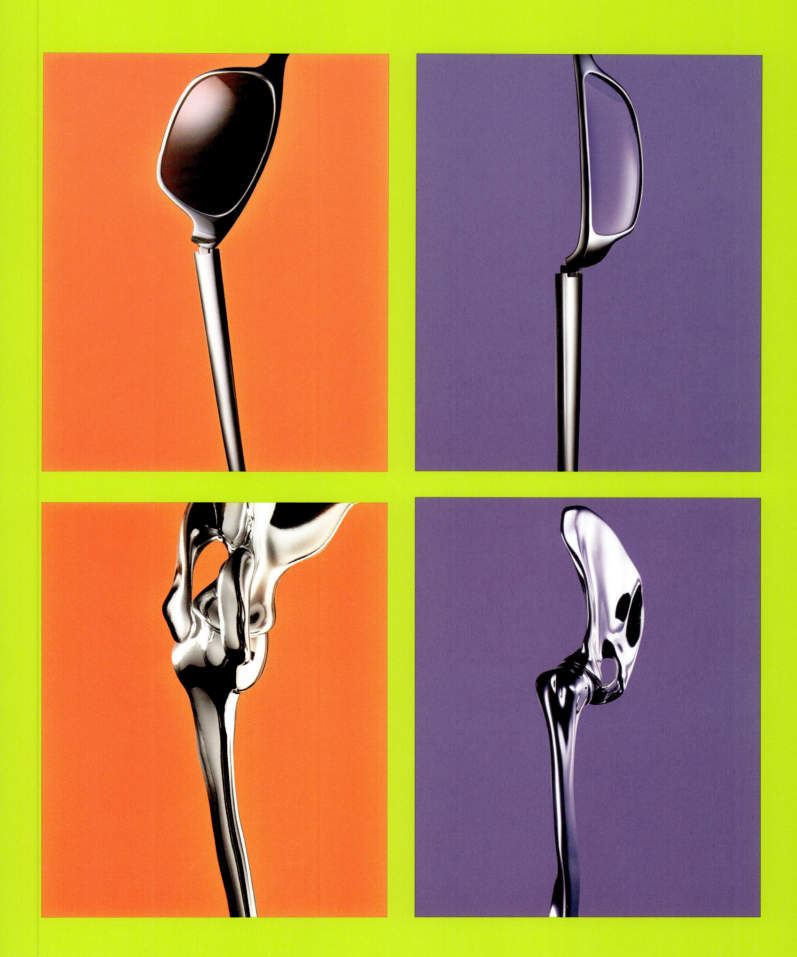

SUPER NAKED XV

Year: 2005 (Project 2004)

Company: Voxan

Voxan is the only motorcycle manufacturer in France. The small company, founded in 1995 by Jacques Gardette, can produce up to a thousand motorcycles per year. All of the models use the same engine, a 996 cc V-twin with fuel injection After it went into liquidation, in June 2010 Voxan was bought by Venturi Automobiles. Starck uses a motorbike, his favourite vehicle, whenever he has to travel more than 150 km, and for Voxan he designed a minimum but meaty 1200 cc model. He describes his Super Naked Xv as "the radical purity of minimalism at the service of brute power. The absolute essence of any motorcycle".

ZIKMU

Year: 2005

Company: Parrot

These loudspeakers called Zikmu have revolutionized traditional acoustic design by using innovative technology capable of immersing users in a total listening experience. And people can share their listening experience with others: all they have to do is place an iPhone or an iPod on top and the sound is reproduced by both loudspeakers. An ultrathin membrane creates subtle vibrations all along the surface so that both medium and high frequencies are faithfully reproduced on both sides of the loudspeakers. Resembling stylized columns, 70 cm in height to optimize the listening of a person seated on a sofa or at a desk, these loudspeakers were created to be compatible with the whole range of latest-generation Apple products. Starck explains that it's really a "self-designed" product, since his intervention was reduced to the bare minimum: simply a support for the advanced technology and at the top a footprint just big enough to accommodate an iPhone or an iPod; below, enough width to hide the bass. Thanks to Bluetooth technology or Wi-Fi the loudspeakers can amplify music from any computer or iPhone without requiring any wiring. Featuring unparalleled aesthetics, Zikmu loudspeakers give sound an almost palpable effect that fills the atmosphere in the same way as perfume does. "With Zikmu", Starck explains, I've succeeded in making the air vibrate". He continues: "These loudspeakers foreshadow the most extreme and innovative technology while involving the least amount of material possible, and at the same time offering the utmost effect: magic!"

MR. IMPOSSIBLE

Year: 2007

Company: Kartell

Material: clear or mass-coloured polycarbonate

Nomina sunt consequentia rerum: indeed this chair is born from the apparently impossible idea of joining two oval polycarbonate shells, i.e. a clear frame and a full-coloured seat, without using glue to do so. The two laser-welded shells give the chair a two-toned as well as a three-dimensional appearance. The shell-like shape endows the product with excellent ergonomics and an inviting appearance. Starck describes it as a chair with an organic design, an extremely clean one formally speaking, which invites the viewer to sit down, inspiring comfort at first sight. There is more than one colour to choose from for the seat, which, thanks to the double-shell effect, has the depth and brilliance of a precious gemstone. Laser-welding has given plastic a whole new nature: it is no longer considered poor material, but as rich as Chinese lacquer.

PRIVÉ
SERIES OF CHAIRS, SOFAS AND BEDS

Year: 2007

Company: Cassina

Materials: aluminium, goose down, steel, expanded polyurethane foam with polyester padding (backrest and armrests), quilted leather (upholstery)

A fully-fledged "family" of different types of seating that also includes beds. The basic frame and legs are made from polished aluminium with visible Schienale leather straps, while the backrest, seat and armrests are made from expanded polyurethane foam with polyester padding. The right or left horizontal armrest acts as a support unit and can either be fixed or is adjustable in height. Cushions filled with goose down come with removable covers and the upholstery features quilted leather. Starck's idea was to create a collection that could be used for having sex in a decent environment, acceptable even for the grandmother who arrives unexpectedly. "I became aware of a glaring inconsistency. Sex is everywhere today. All you have to do is open a magazine or turn on the TV; but oddly enough in the home there is no piece of furniture devoted to sex. We have the right to sit down, eat, sleep, but it's as if we didn't have the right to make love, except in the bedroom. I decided that this inconsistency needed to be solved, and because I'm obsessed with sex I based the project on my own personal experience and designed a collection that favours a woman's comfort and creativity while she's having sex". Starck continues: "Love is everything, sex is everywhere, love is crucial. Sex is light. Sex can also be a game... Furniture has forgotten all about sex. A bed can be fine, but it's a bit boring. A rug will scratch your back. Being uncomfortable is not a duty, especially for a woman. Why not add pleasure to the fantasy of pleasure?... A bit of comfort, but most of all furniture that, thanks to its mobility, versatility, adaptability, allows the user to rediscover a forgotten agility. I think this type of furniture is coherent with future love and its new visions. But how does one make a piece of erotic furniture fit in with one's daily life? What will one's mother-in-law have to say next Sunday? Thanks to its twofold identity and its dual language, Starck's Privé collection is the answer to this paradox: elegance during the day, games at night. Both in the afternoon...Privé invents a new imaginary territory: for love, dedicated to love".

Passion (no. 10),
Privé collection,
Cassina, 2007

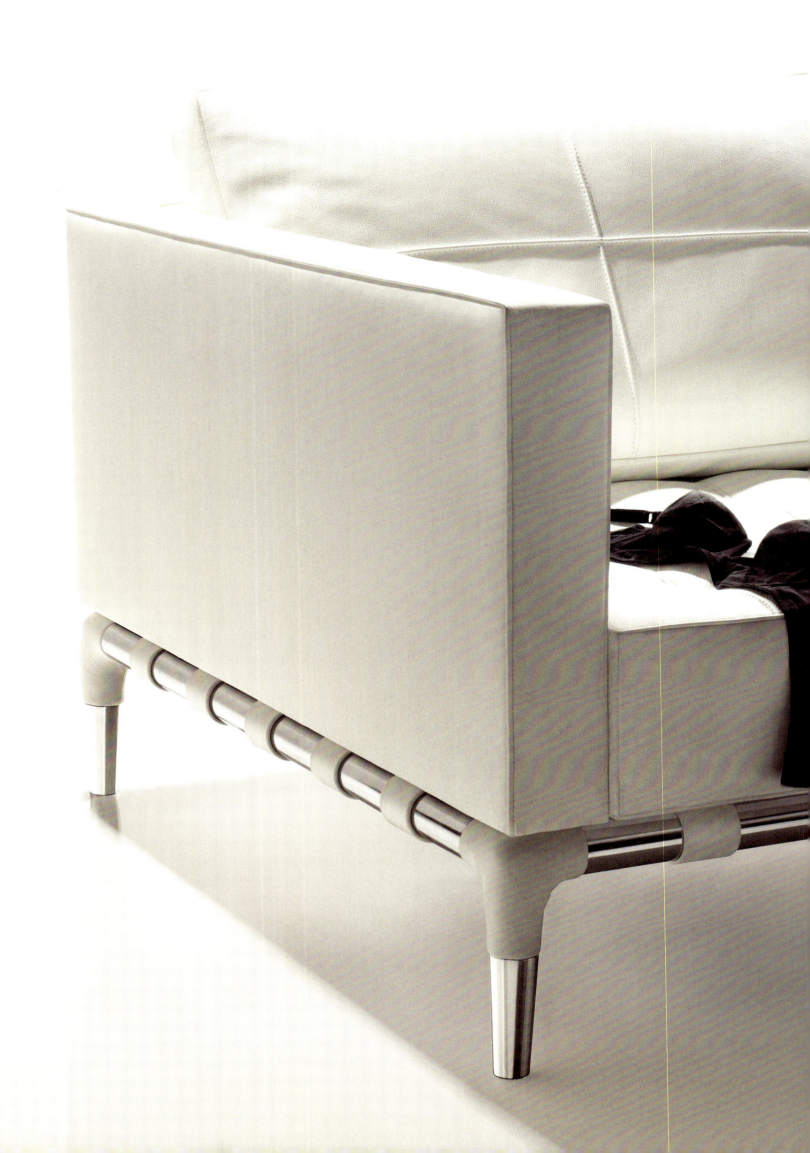

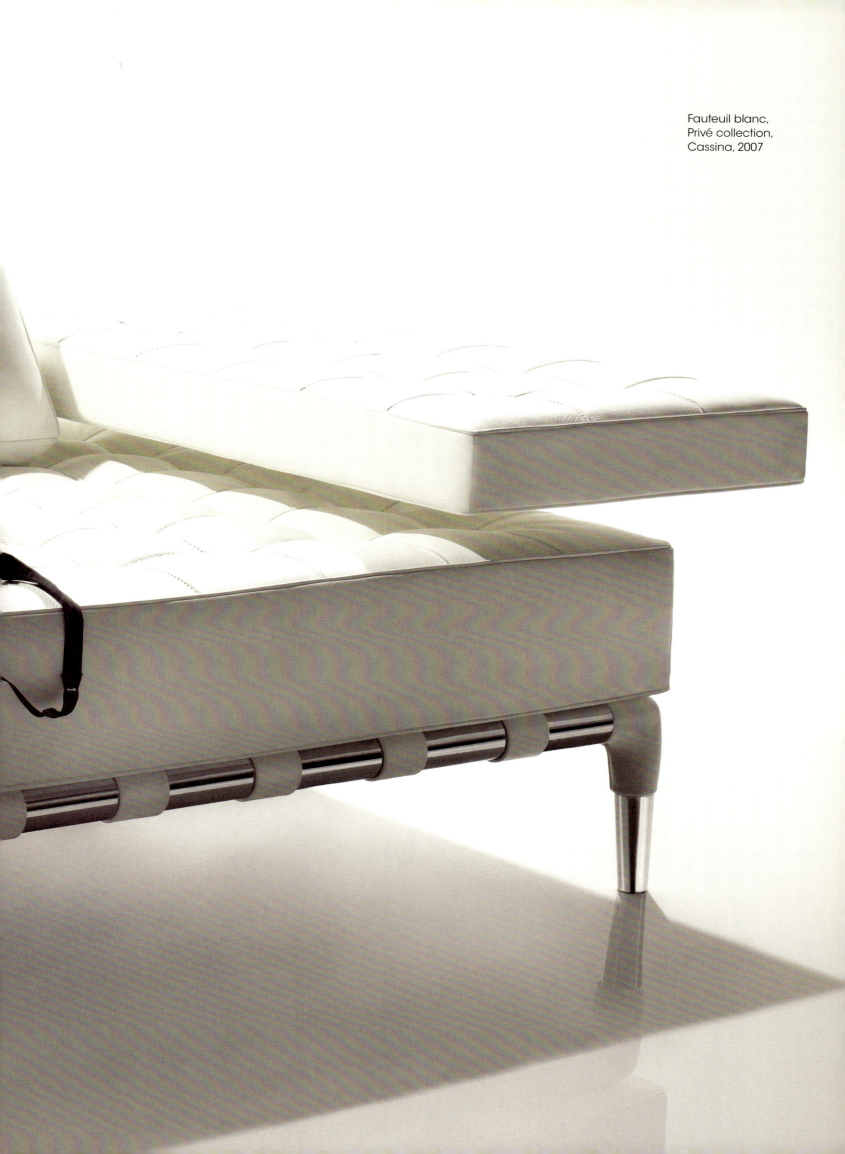

Fauteuil blanc,
Privé collection,
Cassina, 2007

MI MING

Made in collaboration with: Eugeni Quitllet

Year: 2008

Company: XO

Material: polycarbonate

As can be seen from the name the reference is explicit: the classical, timeless Chinese chair. The past is transformed into pure modernity leaving aside any traces of nostalgia thanks to the use of clear polycarbonate. The Mi Ming is solid and comfortable even though it consists of pure reflection. A pure reflection that becomes realistic thanks to the polycarbonate profile that's either mass-coloured or made of birchwood and joins the back to the armrest to embrace the sitter. The Mi Ming, designed, according to Starck, "as a tribute to our masters of the future", combines the transparency of the polycarbonate and the lightness of the gas-assisted injection. Yet another balancing act for Philippe Starck, one where he blends modern design with the ethnic elements of memory, bestowing the product with an image that's immediately captivating. Mi Ming is the new chapter of the project that began with Kartell's Louis Ghost chair. Louis Ghost represents the memory of the Western world, while Mi Ming expresses the traditional Far Eastern one.

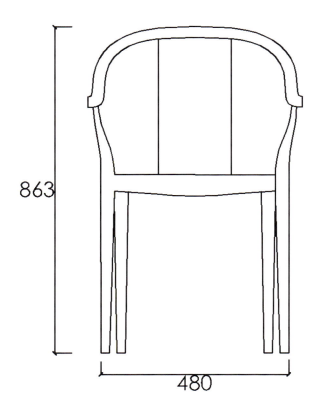

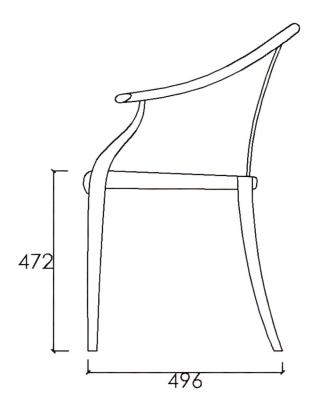

HOBICAT+

Made in collaboration with: Thierry Gaugain

Year: 2009

Builder: Hobie Cat

Philippe Starck is very keen on boats and is proud to own and steer each one of the Hobie Cat models. "Sailing on a Hobie Cat is much more than a passion, it's a religion", Starck says, "the religion of what's minimal". And no one better than Hobie Alter (Ontario, 1933), the man who developed fibreglass surfboards and invented the Hobie Cat, has explored the elegance of the minimal. Starck says that he's a visionary and a precursor. For him minimum is not a choice but the very heart of the project. For the dawning of the third millennium Starck and Thierry Gaugain, with their 5-metre Hobie Cat, decided to make the boat's original design even more radical, so that its use is now more flexible, its assembly and transportation simpler, honing comfort and reducing costs. With Hobie Cat+ Starck offers the opportunity to explore the elegance of the minimal, but intelligence as well.

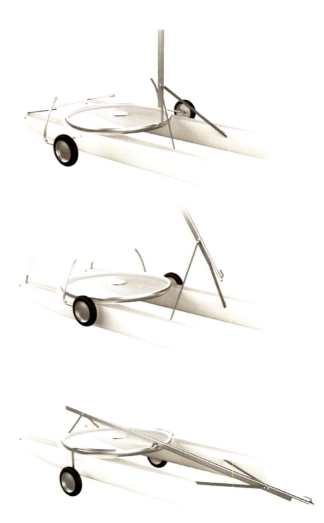

HOME GYM OFFICE

Realized in collaboration with: Eugeni Quitllet

Year: 2009 (project from 2006)

Company: Alias

The collection includes Barbell, weights made of a chrome-plated brass alloy with thermoplastic slip-resistant rubber inserts; Multipurpose Hook, a rope and accessory hook that comes in white, black or metallic titanium polycarbonate; an adjustable-length rope for skipping made of PVC or leather and shiny aluminium handles with an ergonomic grip; Gym Mat, a foldable mattress with a dark brown leather surface, closed-cell expanded polyurethane filling, and slip-resistant black rubber bottom; and Rack, made of chrome steel rod with a steel sheet base and a rubber stopper ring. The project marks Starck's beginnings in the area of wellness and inaugurates his collaboration with Alias. These elegant and innovative pieces are conceived to guarantee a more confident approach to fitness, fostering its introduction into everyday life, especially at home as not everyone can go to the gym. Starck's words are: "Life is something impossible that we need to carry out. Better to prolong it. That's why we must love life, love ourselves, at least 15 minutes a day. At work and at home. Just a few exercises and good posture, elegant, of course..."

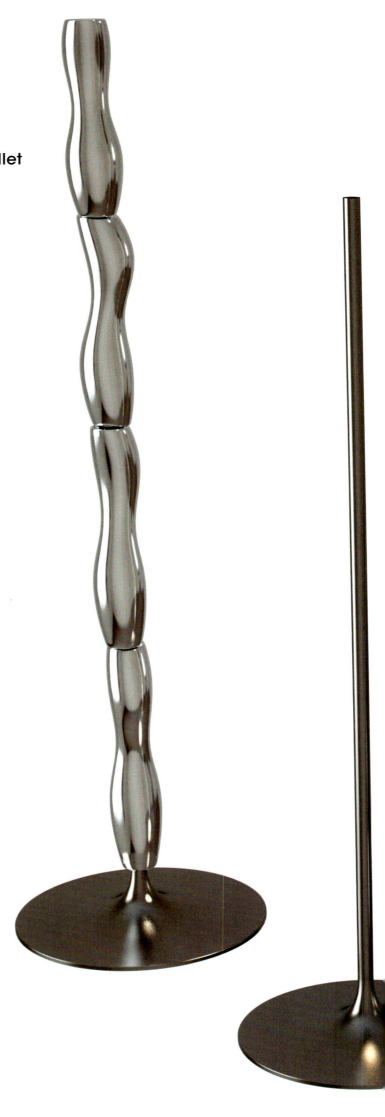

LA FEUILLE D'EAU

Year: 2009

Fondation France-libertés

The Feuille d'eau was designed by Philippe Starck for France Libertés founded by Danielle Mitterand in 1986 to support the recent campaign that says water is a public asset. (The feuille d'eau is the leitmotif visible on the capitals of Cistercian abbeys.) It's a flat bottle with a message written inside that's magnified by the water: "As the common asset of humanity, water is priceless". The aim of the project is to encourage people to drink tap water and to have the Feuille d'eau with them at all times. To make it easier for the water drinker to slip the bottle into a pocket or a handbag, to make it more natural to use, the bottom of the bottle isn't flat but cut at a slant. Another reason why it's flat is so that it won't clutter tables used for meetings. It can be bought for 5 Euros on the France Libertés website, 2 of which go to the foundation.

LIGHT PHOTON

Made in collaboration with: Thierry Gaugain

Year: 2009

Company: Flos with Blackbody

Featuring OLED light sources the lamp is made from thin layers of organic material that produce a white monochromatic light when electrically charged. OLED is a flat light source, similar to a luminous film that can be touched with one's hands, contrary to the sources currently available, including LEDs. OLEDs, which are easily disposed of in recycling systems, can perhaps be described as the most ecological of all light sources. "It's the first lighting fixture in the world that uses organic LEDs", Starck says, "It's the most with the least. It expresses the absolute elegance of a design that works by subtraction. This lamp, which uses up very little energy, doesn't even have a switch; to turn it on all you have to do is make a gesture in the air". Thanks to the concision of its design Light Photon egregiously lends itself to expressing an idea that's very dear to Starck, that of the gradual dematerialization of the world. Indeed, his words are: "True, nothing really exists. Einstein had predicted it, others have said it. No more materiality, no more time intervals…Our lives can be summed up in a quantistic addition… But photons, never! Those do exist. So let's narrow them down, laminate them…They hardly exist anymore, that's how thin they are, they, too, have vanished. Then how can we explain this miracle? OLEDs. The new lighting unit manufactured by Flos, created by Starck and Gaugain with Blackbody. Photons that are as flat as can be. Anything less would be impossible!

S+ARCK® **WITH BALLANTYNE**

Year: 2009

Company: Ballantyne

Material: "technical" cashmere

With this new collection of cashmere clothing Starck declares that he has "explored a new territory of elegance and intelligence". The collection, which features many interesting details, such as the bias-cut sleeve edges that facilitate ergonomy, is made up of 30 pieces for men and 30 for women for a basic line that rises over and above fashion. It's made from yarn that's exclusively spun in the Ballantyne factory in Innerleithen, Scotland. Cashmere treated by highly technological procedures (combined with other "technical" fabrics") is used to make these clothing items. Silk linings are featured in the lighter garments. Jackets and coats come with detachable teddy bear waistcoats that make them ideal in cold weather. The pockets are camoflauged so as to preserve the purity of the design. Jackets and pullovers feature double-face hoods in contrasting colours. The rigorous cut is livened up by the soft colours of the lining. The collection debuted on 16 June 2009 at Pitti Immagine Uomo with Philippe Starck as star guest. Starck doesn't see himself as a designer here; rather, his plan is to develop timeless items capable of being passed down from mother to daughter. Cashmere is a precious fiber and it deserves to be inherited. By creating a design that rises above what's in style, Starck has launched the idea of clothing as a value to be passed on.

PERSONAL INVISIBLE WIND TURBINE

Year: 2010 (Project 2004)

Company: Pramac

Produced by the Tuscany-based firm Pramac which specializes in manufacturing electric generators and parts for photovoltaic systems, this small wind turbine designed by Philippe Starck is meant to solve two problems: it will allow private individuals to use wind as a source of energy, and it will dissimulate the cumbersome and aesthetically polluting aspect of wind power generators since it's completely transparent. A prototype for the turbine was first displayed in Milan in 2008 in the Università Statale's Filarete courtyard as part of the Furniture Fair's Interni event: the very small (less than 50 cm in height), graceful, quiet square object featured a vertical rotation axis in order to make it independent from the wind and allow it to exploit turbulence as well.

The project was realized in 2011 thanks to Pramac. It is the least expensive personal wind turbine on the market. Because it's made of see-through plastic the wind turbine can be discreetly placed on a roof, and is in line with Starck's idea of immateriality, an idea he adamantly supports. He concludes: "I designed a very special windmill: the first almost invisible wind turbine". The item is one of Starck's eco-compatible designs, an issue that he's especially sensitive to. After launching Democratic Design, it is through this product that Starck deals with the theme of democratic ecology so as to develop a series of objects that are ecological, accessible, and easy to find on the market. This is his first, but there are others on the way.

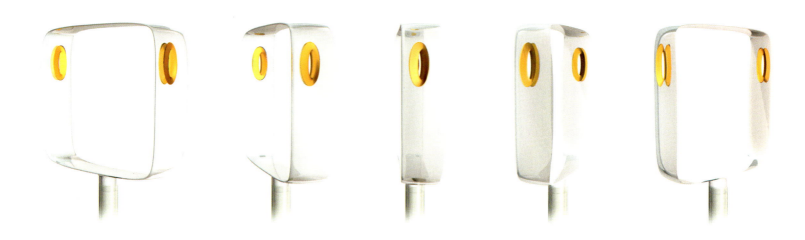

LOU READ

Year: 2011

Company: Driade

Materials: resin (frame), full grain leather (upholstery)

It's a chair that's used for reading, as well as a tribute to Lou Reed (whose name has been deliberately modified), the legendary singer, and a friend of Starck, who often listens to Lou's music while he's creating. The long anatomically shaped backrest resembles a human back. The resin-moulded frame is upholstered with full grain leather that's glued sheath-like directly onto it. The backrest, which resembles a woman's back, tapers towards the svelte waistline, softening as it gets to the armrests, to provide a comfortable sitting position. Rather like a woman in love this chair has its arms outstretched in what appears to be an embrace, and at the glance of an eye it gives the impression of being extremely comfortable. Its accentuated design makes this a "signature" piece, capable of standing out in the contemporary design scenario. The chair was designed for the Royal Manceau Hotel in Paris, also entirely designed by Starck, and the place where he and Lou Reed usually meet.

NET

Year: 2011

Company: Flos

Material: aluminium

"When the iPad, a source of information, becomes a source of light".
Thanks to Net the iPad as a source of information now doubles as a source of light. Net's design is totally radical, just a thin polished aluminium support and a docking connection atop the LED fixture for an iPad, iPhone or iPod. The light source is strong, as much as 28 Top LED 3000K. Net is an efficient table lamp that satisfies our day-to-day need for information, entertainment and especially that of being connected with the rest of the world at any time and wherever we may be.

ZARTAN

Made in collaboration with: Eugeni Quitllet

Year: 2011

Company: Magis

"From head to toe Zartan is a completely natural chair. High ecological technology explores the potentials of bamboo, linen, canvas...so that we can understand what tomorrow will bring" (Philippe Starck). Zartan is a completely natural chair. The compression-moulded shell is made from a totally new natural fibre composite. The injection-moulded legs are instead a mix of natural fibres and "plastic" of plant origin. Starck has deliberately chosen a minimal design to begin a new chapter in the history of industrial design: natural material injected like plastic into a mould. Zartan is the first chair made from injection-moulded 100% natural fibre. Magis accompanies the designer in this new adventure, a company that's specialized in injection-moulded products that thanks to Starck can now boast the use of totally natural composites. A highly experimental process will be used to manufacture the chair which is still in the process of being defined.

Interview

Paris, 29 June 2011, 3 p.m.

From the top:
Philippe Starck on his "bleue";
Philippe Starck aged 14 in an
Abarth; Gérard and Philippe
on the wings of a Starck plane

An empty white room. Just a round white table and some white chairs. Coming in from the outside is the rumbling sound of the traffic on the Trocadero. Jasmine, Philippe's wife, still glowing from the birth of their baby girl Justice, lends a hand and types things out on the computer. Both iPhone and iPad are turned on so as not to miss a single word. In some ways to talk about Philippe Starck is to do him an injustice because it means focusing on the past of someone who only looks to the future. Design makes sense if it's a process that is seen as continually changing and not as an abacus of material things, which should all be thrown out.

The interview, which is an intermission in the short sequence of a here and now that moves towards a tomorrow, does him justice. Philippe is focused when he answers. He listens to each question carefully. He weighs up each and every word. His answers are exact, assertive, final. Not opinions but sharply chiselled statements uttered with firm conviction. The questions are deliberately mundane so that he can reply with that special vision, his own anti-conventional and courageous truth, not just about his work but about life as well.

Cristina Morozzi What is it about your projects that you'd like to save?

Philippe Starck I wouldn't save any of them because projects are material. What I would like to save of my work is just the viewpoint, the spirit, the rationale, a struggle, a rebellion, a poem , a mood and the weaknesses.

C.M. And what would you like to throw out?

P.S. Theoretically everything should be thrown out: there's no reason to be concerned about materiality. Materiality transpires, materiality stinks, materiality sweats, materiality moves. Investing in materiality is a bad investment. There's no history. There's no reason to save it.

C.M. Do you like fashion?

P.S. I like fashion when it offers pleasure. Perhaps in the past it gave women pleasure. Today it's an object of destruction. The commercialism and cynicism that enliven its over-rapid mutation are machines that make people dumb and drive them crazy. Our world can now no longer afford so much materiality being thrown out the window every two months (with all the collections, inter-collections, etc.). Luckily some ideas, which we believe to be modern, are neither modern nor eternal. The death of fashion is already planned. It will happen very soon.

C.M. Do you go to the cinema, to the theatre?

PS: The cinema, the theatre and all the performances that one goes to see to relax are certainly beautiful and interesting things, but they are completely alien to me. I'm already pretty busy trying to nurture the dreams I have in the daytime as well as at night. I don't need to go and see other people's dreams on a big screen.

C.M. Do you watch TV?

P.S. I don't watch TV, nor do I watch other screens. It's not a question of racism. I simply don't have time to. What's more, my autistic nature keeps me away from all forms of understanding and learning.

C.M. Are you autistic?

P.S. Ara, my daughter, found quite an accurate expression—she says I'm a modern autistic.

C.M. Many geniuses are autistic.

P.S. Well then I'm the only person who's autistic but *isn't* a genius!

C.M. Car, motorbike, or bicycle?

P.S. For 5 kilometres a good pair of shoes. For 15 kilometres a good bicycle. For 150 kilometres a good motorcycle, the vehicle I prefer. For everything else an airplane. Cars never, but boats all the time.

C.M. Are you interested in sports? If so, which is your favourite sport?

P.S. I'm not equipped with the software used for sports or races. My only race is against myself and my life. All other forms of play or hobbies seem to be completely useless to me. Maybe they're lacking in poetry. The truth is I don't know and I'm not interested.

C.M. Are you a fan?

P.S. I'm not a fan of anything, except of the woman I love, my wife, and of all of us, human beings and their genius.

C.M. What do you like to read?

P.S. I love so many books that I wouldn't be able to talk about them all. But I have the ambition and the pretence to recognize true literature, a rarity in the mass of publications, and of finding endless joy therein. My only drug is literature...

C.M. Are you a member of any social networks? Are you on Facebook?

P.S. I will never be a member of Facebook. I have no interest in doing such a thing. All I see is frustration. It's a disturbing symptom of our society.

C.M. Do you listen to music and if so which kind? Rock, classical, pop, middle of the road?

P.S. I am inside music. Music is a part of me. It's more than an obsession. It's in my DNA. I hear sounds, I hear noises. Everything produces music and I am constantly composing it in my head. I possess an internal sort of musical software, permanent and parallel. And sometimes it makes me deaf.

C.M. Which authors would you say are your reference points, your legends, in literature, art, design, architecture, music?

P.S. I have no masters. I have no models. In general I'm attracted to scientists and their way of thinking. Their explorations and their work fascinates me. Scientists are my only guides.

C.M. What are you missing?

P.S. My life: because of a lack of confidence in myself and a form of weakness, paradoxical for a man generally judged to be very strong. I'm certain about unimportant details and totally lost when it comes to important decisions. I would have liked to do something for the good of humanity that could have saved lives. And instead all I know how to do is make toothbrushes.

C.M. How do you explain your success?

P.S. My success is, first of all, something that doesn't interest me, perhaps because I'm not aware of it. As I live in a sort of total autarchy I'm not familiar with the sides of society that could reflect my success. Caring for my ego and my desires, it's a notion that doesn't concern me. If we could only consider the results of the projects best-received by my sentimental tribe we would understand that this is the way it is because they speak of other things and because they point to roads that are better than the ones we have at our disposal.

C.M. Do you love solitude or do you prefer to be in the company of others?

P.S. I flee from solitude in terror because, alas, I know I am a loner. My life is a constant struggle to survive the evil of solitude.

C.M. How does one seduce the public, the customers, people in general, women in particular?

P.S. If there's any seduction involved it's absolutely involuntary. Because I don't love myself I don't understand how others can love me. Perhaps this paradox and this naiveté are what reveal a form of purity and generate the impression of extreme rigour, extreme honesty. Rigour and honesty are, perhaps, my only qualities.

C.M. Who would you point to as being your possible heir in design?

P.S. My way of working and my way of living keep me from knowing what others do. I don't even have enough time to work on my own projects, so how can I be interested in those of others? I don't know who my heir might be, but most of all I don't wish it upon him or her. Each generation has to be better than the one that came before. Legacies have no reason for being.

C.M. What's your favourite food?

P.S. My favourite food is really an action: going to the fish and vegetables market with a huge bag. Once I get home I let everything spill out onto the table, open up a bottle of organic wine without sulfites and eat everything almost raw.

C.M. Seaside or mountains?

P.S. The seaside of course. The mountains are a predefined sort of landscape that disturbs me and doesn't let me think. The sea is the terrestrial call of a form of infinity that always remains the best question.

C.M. Does design have a reason for being?

P.S. Design, if it isn't an instrument of seduction that fosters consumption and hyper-consumption,

but rather an instrument of justice, honesty, validity, should be pursued. Little does it matter for the few years I have left to live what sort of design my design is. Between dematerialization and bionics, material is destined to disappear and objects will no longer be designed because they'll either be waves or our own bodies. Future designers will be dieticians or gym teachers.

C.M. Do you think that indignation is a sentiment that should be cultivated?

P.S. Up until six months ago indignation was an interesting word, even if, alas, it represented passiveness more than action. The time we spend being indignant could be used to create and fight. For the past few months indignation has been used by politicized apolitical figures who, although respectable for their needs, their suffering and their urgencies, deceived by the media have muddled up many battles. Whether right or wrong they are capable of doing good and bad. Indignation is meant to shake things up but the media get mixed up in it by making the true meaning of things get lost. To change you have to fight. Today we find ourselves before a magma of frustrations that unfortunately cannot be used for evolution or revolution.

C.M. Are you a pessimist?

P.S. Not at all. I'm clear-headed.

C.M. An optimist then?

P.S. No a realist and a Utopist. Utopia is the only reality.

C.M. Do you have a sweet tooth?

P.S. I'm a monk with a sweet tooth. Theoretically, I live in a form of extreme personal austerity, enlivened by the world of my interests, accompanied,

however, by a form of greediness for the exploration of new foods.

C.M. What does a journey mean to you?

P.S. Travelling is very important because it has been the biggest disaster of my life. I spent 40 years travelling by airplane every single day. I wonder what my past life would have been like on the ground, without jet lag, spending time with my family. The movement of matter and bodies is in some ways a defeat. The imaginary journey is instead always a conquest because it represents the essence of man and his diversity from animals.

C.M. How do you define luxury?

PS: Luxury means being able to recognize real qualities, whatever they are, at whatever price.

C.M. Are you bulimic with information, or do you prefer to keep your head free?

P.S. Both. My head is completely free because I refuse to listen to the information in the media. But I thrive on unconscious micro-data released randomly by society. I listen to the collective subconscious more than to consciousness. This allows me to freely manipulate my magma.

C.M. Reason or sentiment?

P.S. First of all, passion, forever and always. But if it is filtered through a rigorous grid of needs it will be more passionate, more interesting and more solid.

C.M. Vasari or Leon Battista Alberti?

P.S. In theory, Leon Battista Alberti, as he represents rigour. I'm not interested in Renaissance art but in the Renaissance itself, its utopias, its social conquests, its politics, its ideas. The Renaissance is above all a state of mind. I don't deal with art.

C.M. Not even contemporary art?

P.S. Rather more, but I try to keep it away from me as much as possible. Today art is a great supermarket driven by venality. I am eagerly waiting for the bubble to burst.

C.M. Which qualities are essential for a good designer?

P.S. As I'm not a real designer I don't know what the qualities to be one are. I have the impression that every job requires generosity first of all, and therefore respect for the people on the receiving end of the job, but even more importantly the awareness of deserving to exist.

C.M. What's your secret to make all the most different styles come together, for example Fornasetti with Riccardo Dalisi, Venini with Emeco?

P.S. These stylistic combinations are purely functional. It's a way of building places that have the same diversity and richness as life. It's a way to avoid seeing things as either black or white, one-track thinking, but above all it's a way to create fruitful short circuits and surprises that are no more than a psychological game. These are stories of varying origins and different cultures, where people find memories and hopes. These cross-pollinations help to broaden the mind.

C.M. How many people are there working in your study?

P.S. I've done everything possible to stay small. I'd like to be alone with my wife. Unfortunately, society won't allow for such light structures. I try to stay minimal, overseeing things and trying to be very rigorous. There are ten of us more or less. If the number were higher I'd feel like some minister of creation and I'd be so bored that I wouldn't even come to the office any more, which would neither be good nor wise. Clearly, I prefer people's qualities over quantity. Which means that I design almost everything personally. Everything that works comes straight out of my head, everything that's wrong is my work too.

C.M. What do you think of Italian companies?

P.S. After having worked for the whole world, after having learned to recognize the qualities and the flaws in every nationality, I can assure you that Italian entrepreneurs are the most efficient of all. That blend of innate culture, courage, boldness, pleasure, human elegance, intelligence and technology make them the most balanced businesspeople and the ones with the greatest sense of justice. They are one-of-a-kind.

C.M. Which of your projects best represent you?

P.S. Each project is a stage, a rung. You can't let yourself get excited about a rung on a ladder. What counts is that the ladder lead somewhere. Each realization was important, both for its force and its weakness, because the two qualities are the parameters of understanding that make evolution and progress possible.

Porte Helicoptère, 2011

p. 111
75-metre Yacht with sliding
door, work in progress, 2010

Critique

A great deal has been written about him in the media of all types and categories: design magazines, women's magazines, weeklies, current affairs publications and daily newspapers. He was one of the first designers to be talked about in the daily news. Journalists queue up just to interview him. His work has attracted the interest of design critics, sociologists, philosophers and anthropologists. He confesses that he's famous because it is through his creations that he expresses the essence of design, which is none other than the instrument he uses to give a voice to his own Self. He doesn't limit himself to the subject of design, but is also and above all concerned with well-being and love. He has learned that people will allow themselves to be mesmerized by stories and thus makes lavish use of them. For each of his projects, akin to a skilful director, he sets up a play, reciting the dialogues that might take place between the objects and the users, between the designer and his inventions. To get an idea of his published work, you'd best get some scales and weigh them in kilos, that's how many publications he's collected. Because he has managed to impose himself as a star, he collects interviews during which he dishes out pearls of wisdom. He loves to philosophize and has the gift of being to the point, singling out the crux of the matter which he handles with great skill. It's not easy to quibble with him: always ready with his explanations and anecdotes he's the one who actually fills the pens of critics and journalists with ink. Always the smooth talker he uses persuasive words to present his designs, which are on the scene from start to finish. His words are the best companions for his products. Suffice it to read the descriptions of his projects in the breviary-like book bound in pink leather with silver gilt-edged pages published by the Centre George Pompidou on the occasion of his solo show in 2003, to realize that there's not much else to say and that, at last, design has abandoned its sectorial language to instead speak the language that is common to us all. No captions, no technical explanations but rather charming fairy tales to be read aloud to children too. Starck is a great communicator: he speaks to explain that his projects are instruments of reconciliation and that, before being objects for use, they are media that transmit healthy emotions, good vibrations and different kinds of messages: about love, tenderness; they are philosophical messages, messages about well-being, etc. There's never any need to decipher what he has to say: he knows how to make himself understood and be admired by every category of person, design expert as well as common folk, because he possesses the art of arousing wonder and the gift of surprising. Words about his designs are often superfluous, also because Starck himself has so much to say about them. Starck has made design glamorous, bestowing upon the genre the same fanatical attraction that you find in rock music and movie stars. There's always something mysterious and undecipherable about charm, that doesn't just concern form, the surface, harmony, balance, the exactness of the geometry, but rather magnetic waves of a sort that generate flashes or, as Donald A. Norman, a professor of psychology and cognitive science at Northwestern University, puts it "purely visceral reactions", such as for example the Juicy Salif citrus-squeezer manufactured by Alessi, which he bought on impulse. In *Emotional Design: Why We Love (or Hate) Everyday Things* (New York: Basic Books, 2004) he asks himself why a bizarre object like the Juicy Salif is also so delightful. Fortunately, he says, Khaslavsky and Shedroff have done an analysis and provided an answer (1999): Because it "entices by diverting attention [...] delivers surprising novelty [...] goes beyond obvious needs and expectations [so that it] becomes something else entirely [because it] creates an instinctive response [...] espouses values or connections to personal goals [...] transform[ing] the routine act of juicing an orange into a special experience [because] it promises to make an ordinary action extraordinary. It also promises to raise the status of the owner to a higher level of sophistication for recognizing its qualities. [...] While the juicer doesn't necessarily teach the user anything new about juice or juicing, it does teach the lesson that even ordinary things in life can be interesting and that design can enhance living. It also teaches to expect wonder where it is unexpected. [...] Every time it is used it reminds the user of its elegance and approach to design". In 1987 (issue no. 14) the French magazine *Intramuros*, created and directed by Chantal Hamaide, dedicated a long article to Philippe Starck written by Sophie Tasma Anargyros. As usual Starck holds his own and launches the concept of "the right objects". About this "rightness" he says: "I could go on talking for hours and say that it concerns the sphericity of my way of working. There are a number of parameters that can't be quantified and that must agree with each other. If the product doesn't realize the cohesion, i.e. the sphere, then it isn't perfect". By the end of the meeting Sophie jots down with some amazement that "the only truly international designer, who will unquestionably be one of the most relevant in the history of interior design, works in a greenhouse at the back of a garden furnished with anonymous pieces of furniture on a table pushed up against the window in the middle of endless sketches, drawings and models with two young assistants who look more like rock singers" and that for the whole time "he laughed his heart out like a little boy who's played a prank that no one has noticed yet". In 1998, again in *Intramuros* and once more through Sophie Tasma Anargyros's pen, Starck launched a few of his most famous slogans, such as: "Intelligence is female; progress is a romantic notion; we don't need to kill to survive; civism is avant-garde". He deals with the theme of the moral market, goes back to that of the right product, and puts forward the notion of "lightweight compassion." "Not religious compassion", he says, "but individual compassion, lightweight, uncommon, the creator of surprises, the opposite of theatricality. We need to rehabilitate modesty and above all goodness. But since altruism no longer works, we need to talk about a selfish goodness that brings out truly personal benefits".

Enrico Baleri, who brought Philippe Starck's work to Italy, talks about him in *Progetto discreto*, memoirs published on the occasion of the designer's show at the Palazzo Municipale in Bergamo (19 May - 6 June, 2009): the "Café Costes" he writes "is the work that made Starck famous in no time at all. In the middle of the café is a large, actually a huge clock, two and a half metres across, so you can feel time passing by; there's something Proustian about it, it's like being in a station [...]. The focal point at the Café Costes is the clock, a clock that Starck drew on a sheet of paper, a sketch for the artisan who was going to make it. He drew it in his own way, in just a minute he'd made a circle, then instead of numbers he'd marked the four cardinal points and then he added four other signs in between them, unusual signs [...]. The result being that it's impossible to tell what time it is as the clock is completely incomprehensible!"

Marie Laure Jousset, who was the design director at the Centre Georges Pompidou and curator of the Starck solo show (2003) at the time, in her introduction to *Starck Explications* (Paris: Éditions du Centre Pompidou, 2003) reveals that "this designer who has turned his name into a brand and who has always behaved like a rock star, even from the very beginning, actually manifests a sort of shyness, a malaise when he has to display his work [...]". She continues: "His radical decision not to let the public see any of his works is supported by his desire to take this opportunity to delve more deeply into the strange relations he weaves with the imaginary, so as to be able to explain these objects without either filters or intermediaries, convinced that all the sources of his work originate from his unconscious". She then notes that Starck is someone who "loves to open doors, ask questions, annoy, be amazed by and amaze others. The legends that accompany his work are those of Faust, Pandora's box and the sorcerer's apprentice".

In *Scritti su Starck*, Christine Colin, design critic, inspector at the Délégation aux arts plastiques and head of the design collection at the National

Lan Restaurant,
Peking, 2007

Collection of Contemporary Art, who published her first book on Starck in 1988 (Mardaga), in *Scritti su Starck* says: "Everything leads us to believe that Starck the designer was not born in France, but in science fiction. Wasn't one of the first things he did that of naming his company "Ubik" (the title of a novel by Philip K. Dick written in 1969) and of giving everything he made starting from the early 1980s the names of the characters from the novel?" (V. Guillaume (ed.), *Scritti su Starck*, Milan: Postmedia, 2004). Valérie Guillaume says that Starck "effects an iconoclastic synthesis that refuses the current hierarchy established between cultural references, and instead blends together pieces of furniture that are popular, artisanal, industrial, designer or rustic, originals or copies. Using the aesthetic processes of collage and montage, the designer experiments with the issues of the continuous, discontinuous, continuous, surplus, addition, absence, conceal-ment, filling to the brim, unity and multiplicity [...] This play space refers back to a physical or mental activity whose sole purpose in the consciousness of the person involved is the pleasure that it brings about" (V. Guillaume, *op. cit.*).

The relationship between modern essentialness and Deco elegance recalls the great Patrick Chareau

and his ability to combine the softness of elegance and the hardness of metal" (V. Guillaume, *op. cit.*). But as dealing with Starck critically does not mean studying object design alone but a more general design that concerns the designer's own persona, the most pertinent exegesis of the "phenomenon" is provided by the philosopher Michael Onfray, the founder of the Popular University of Caen in 2002 and a theoretician on hedonism. "A designer, of course", he argues, "obviously an architect, the creator of forms and objects straight off [...] but also an artist, someone who proceeds as though he were a demiurge who powerfully transforms all that he touches [...] who transfigures the real, wipes out the separation between the museum object and the everyday one. With him, thanks to him, we can inhabit our own home as though it were a museum [...]. In the game suggested by Starck objects are humanized and humans objectified, animals are mineralized and vegetables hominized [...]. Thanks to Starck, the most common object is charged with initiatory force and value. It intercedes as something more than itself, a testimony to what overrides it, but that nonetheless remains inside it [...]. Starck points to paths that reconcile aesthetics, ethics and politics" (V. Guillaume, *op. cit.*).

Selected
References

P. Renaud, *Philippe Starck: Mobilier 1970-1987*, Marseille: Michel Aveline Editeur, 1987.

C. Colin, *Starck*, Wavre: Pierre Mardaga Editeur, 1988.

F. Bertone, *L'architettura*, Florence: Octavo, 1994.

P. Mello, *Progetti in movimento. Philippe Starck*, Florence: Festina Lente, 1997.

C. Lloyd-Morgan, *Starck*, Paris. Adam Biro, 1999.

F. Sweet, *Philippe Starck Subverchic Design*, New York: Watson-Guptill, 1999.

V. Guillaume, *Ecrits sur Starck*, Paris: Centre Georges Pompidou, 2003.

P. Starck, *Starck Explications*, Paris: Centre Georges Pompidou, 2003.

Starck, Köln: Taschen, 2004.

P. Starck, K. Hoppen, J. Jagger, M. Wanders, J. Hitchcox, *Interiors by You*, London: Goodman Books, 2009.

Philippe Starck The thousands of projects—complete or forthcoming—his global fame and tireless protean inventiveness should never distract from Philippe Starck's fundamental vision: Creation, whatever form it takes, must improve the lives of as many people as possible. Starck vehemently believes this poetic and political duty, rebellious and benevolent, pragmatic and subversive, should be shared by everyone and he sums it up with the humour that has set him apart from the very beginning: "No one has to be a genius, but everyone has to participate." His precocious awareness of ecological implications, his enthusiasm for imagining new lifestyles, his determination to change the world, his love of ideas, his concern with defending the intelligence of usefulness—and the usefulness of intelligence—has taken him from iconic creation to iconic creation... From the everyday products, furniture and lemon squeezers, to revolutionary mega yachts, hotels that stimulate the senses, phantasmagorical venues and individual wind turbines, he never stops pushing the limits and criteria of contemporary design. His dreams are solutions, solutions so vital that he was the first French man to be invited to the TED conferences (Technology, Entertainment & Design) alongside renowned participants including Bill Clinton and Richard Branson. Inventor, creator, architect, designer, artistic director, Philippe Starck is certainly all of the above, but more than anything else he is an honest man directly descended from the Renaissance artists. (by Jonathan Wingfield)

Cristina Morozzi She works as a journalist, a critic and an art director in the multidisciplinary field of art, fashion and design. For nine years (from 1987 to 1996) she directed the design magazine *Modo.* She has contributed articles to design magazines and newspapers, and she is the author of theoretical texts and monographs (the most recent of these dedicated to Stefano Giovannoni, published by Electa, 2008). A curator of exhibitions, she was also a member of the board for the first Youth Design Biennial in Turin (2009). Together with Stefania Ricci she curated *Salvatore Ferragamo Evolving Legend,* 1928-2008, a tribute to the griffe's eightieth anniversary, held at the Moca in Shanghai and at the Milan Triennale in 2008. In 2009, she curated *L'anima sensibile delle cose* at the Triennale Design Museum. She teaches at the Ecole cantonale d'art de Lausanne and is the art director on behalf of the Skitsch trademark.